D1117662

Nuclear Power: The Market Test

Christopher Flavin

HC
59.
W64
no.57

Worldwatch Paper 57
December 1983

73520

Selections of this paper may be reproduced in magazines and
newspapers with acknowledgment to Worldwatch Institute. The
views expressed are those of the author and do not necessarily
represent those of Worldwatch Institute and its directors, officers
or staff.

©Copyright Worldwatch Institute 1983
Library of Congress Catalog Card Number 83-51433
ISBN 0-916468-56-9

Printed on recycled paper

Table of Contents

Introduction

Nuclear power was considered vital to humanity's future until just a short time ago. Its seemingly infinite potential and the freedom from fossil fuel dependence that it promises made nuclear power seem inevitable. Although issues such as plant safety, waste disposal and the spread of atomic weapons soon created controversy, faith in this energy source among key decision makers remained high throughout the past three decades. Their confidence was based largely on economics. Whatever its other problems, nuclear power was sure to be less expensive than the available alternatives.

Since the late seventies, however, economic viability has joined the list of issues that call into question the future of nuclear power. From state regulatory hearings to the highest levels of national energy planning, the economics of nuclear power has gained center stage. One might expect careful economic analysis to provide some calm amid the fury, but nuclear economics has proved to be almost as hotly disputed as other nuclear issues. Cost estimates frequently vary by a factor of two or more, and economists examining the same issues often reach sharply contrasting conclusions.

Although analysts continue to disagree on many issues, few can doubt that a wide range of economic problems has buffeted nuclear power since the early seventies. Cost overruns on nuclear projects have become endemic and devastating. Figures from utilities and governments in key countries show near-universal increases in the real (inflation-adjusted) cost of nuclear power during the past decade. Nuclear power has lost substantial economic ground compared to coal-fired power—the other main source of new baseload generating capacity in most countries. Only in France and a few other nations are new nuclear plants a less expensive power source than new coal plants, and nowhere is nuclear power economical compared to investment in improved energy efficiency. In addition, dramatic slowdowns in the rates of growth of electricity demand in many nations have eliminated the need for many nuclear plants now under construction.

I would like to thank Peter Bradford, Irvin Bupp, Scott Fenn, S. David Freeman, Charles Komanoff, Amory Lovins and Edward Sullivan for reviewing this manuscript and John Foggle for research assistance in preparing this publication.

6 The major economic assessments on which today's nuclear power programs are based are riddled with errors. But with billion-dollar decisions riding on the outcome, utilities and their customers cannot afford to proceed blindly any further. Developing countries particularly need better information since many have little idea of the financial risks involved in their nascent nuclear programs. Continuing cost increases for nuclear power and a troubled world economy will likely make the economics of nuclear power an increasingly prominent issue in many nations in the next few years.

The economics of nuclear power cannot be separated from other important nuclear issues. Waste disposal and radiation hazards, for instance, have major economic implications. And the need to make nuclear plants safer is at the root of much of the cost increase. These issues are, of course, enormously important on their own, but the economics of nuclear power today will help set the context in which other issues are examined. If nuclear power is cost-effective, some may consider its many risks worth accepting. But if nuclear power is not economical and unlikely to become so, it will be cut back or abandoned, regardless of how the other questions are resolved. The time to make difficult decisions is at hand.

The Selling of Nuclear Power

The eighties were expected to be a glorious decade for nuclear power worldwide. In 1970 the Organisation for Economic Co-operation and Development (OECD) projected that its member nations in Western Europe, North America and Japan would have 568,000 megawatts of nuclear generating capacity by 1985—about half the generating capacity that OECD countries have in all sources combined in 1983. Nuclear power plants were to be built at a rate of over 100 per year during the eighties. The United States alone planned to have 1,200 operating nuclear plants by the end of the century.[1]

Today, just a decade after these bullish nuclear power forecasts, the world is using less than half as much nuclear power as was projected. The nuclear industry's plans have shrunk even more. Estimates for 1990 show nuclear plants supplying only 300,000 to 400,000 megawatts of capacity, compared to the over one million megawatts pro-

"So far in the eighties,
nuclear plant cancellations
have been outrunning
new orders worldwide."

jected in International Atomic Energy Agency documents a decade ago.[2] The largest reductions have been made in the United States, where 87 plants have been canceled since 1975. Major cutbacks have also been made in Western Europe, the Soviet Union and the Third World.

Nuclear power is by no means insignificant, however. As of November 1983, 282 commercial nuclear plants in 25 countries provided 174,000 megawatts of generating capacity—enough to produce about 9 percent of the world's electricity, or 3 percent of total energy. (See Table 1.) In industrial countries the share of electricity supplied by nuclear power varies widely: about 40 percent in France, 17 percent in Japan, 13 percent in the United States, 6 percent in the Soviet Union and zero in nations such as Australia and Denmark that have decided to forego harnessing the atom altogether.[3] In the next three years, over 100 nuclear plants are scheduled to begin operating, boosting global nuclear capacity by 60 percent. The 171 plants now under construction run up a bill of approximately $40 billion each year—not the usual measure of a sick industry.

The large number of plants operating and nearing completion reflect past ambitious plans and investments more than the health of today's industry. So far in the eighties, nuclear plant cancellations have been outrunning new orders worldwide. Unless fortunes shift quickly, the pipeline of new plants will begin to run dry in all but a few countries by the end of the decade. *The Financial Times Energy Economist*, a newsletter of the international energy establishment, reported in early 1983 that, "The day when nuclear power will be the world's leading electricity source now seems to have been postponed indefinitely."[4] To the surprise of many, nuclear power's economic failings are what most jeopardize its future.

Commercial nuclear power has a short history. Although the atom was first fissioned in Germany in 1938, the only real fruits of the nuclear age after a decade and a half were nuclear submarines, some important medical uses of radiation and weapons of mass destruction. The United States and the Soviet Union, which led the world in developing nuclear technologies during the forties and fifties, concentrated their early expertise and funds on weapons development. Civilian nuclear research and development programs were more

Table 1: Worldwide Nuclear Power Commitment, November 1983

Country	Operating		Ordered or Under Construction*		Total Commitment	
	(number)	(megawatts)	(number)	(megawatts)	(number)	(megawatts)
United States	77	60,026	64	70,376	141	130,402
France	31	21,778	31	34,520	62	56,298
West Germany	12	9,806	17	19,516	29	29,322
Japan	25	16,652	15	12,649	40	29,301
Soviet Union	34	18,915	11	9,880	45	28,795
Canada	12	6,622	12	8,710	24	15,332
Great Britain	34	9,273	8	5,115	42	14,388
Spain	6	3,820	7	6,801	13	10,621
Sweden	10	7,300	2	2,110	12	9,410
South Korea	1	556	8	6,710	9	7,266
Belgium	5	3,450	2	2,000	7	5,450
Switzerland	4	1,940	3	3,007	7	4,947
Taiwan	4	3,110	2	1,814	6	4,924
Czechoslovakia	2	880	8	3,520	10	4,400
Italy	3	1,285	3	2,004	6	3,289
Brazil	-	—	3	3,116	3	3,116
East Germany	5	1,830	2	880	7	2,710
India	4	804	6	1,320	10	2,124
Argentina	1	335	2	1,292	3	1,627
Rest of World	12	5,205	21	14,044	33	19,249
World Total	282	173,587	227	209,384	509	382,971

*Includes over ten plants where construction has been suspended.
Source: *Nuclear News*, August 1983, Atomic Industrial Forum and press reports.

modest, but enthusiasm ran high. To many people nuclear power seemed to provide the key to the world's future. It would supply infinite amounts of energy indefinitely and remove many of the constraints under which humanity had struggled for millennia. The

"The U.S. Government
was willing to go where the Fortune 500
feared to tread."

Chancellor of the University of Chicago predicted that, "Heat will be so plentiful that it will be used to melt snow as it falls."[5]

In the early fifties both the United States and the Soviet Union greatly accelerated their R&D programs to commercialize nuclear power.[6] Among the reactor designs tested were gas-cooled reactors, molten salt breeder reactors and two kinds of light water reactors. Major technical improvements led to the world's first electricity-producing reactors: a small breeder plant built in the United States in 1951, and a five-megawatt light water plant built in the Soviet Union in 1954. Also successful were the nuclear-powered submarines developed in a crash U.S. Navy program, headed by the hard-driving Admiral Hyman Rickover. Light water reactors that powered these submarines were the models for the first true nuclear power plant, built at Shippingport, Pennsylvania in 1957.

Efforts in other countries to develop nuclear power in the fifties were hampered by an early superpower monopoly on nuclear technologies and fuel supplies. Countries that nevertheless began substantial nuclear power programs include Canada, Great Britain, France and West Germany, each pursuing its own approach to nuclear technology. Unexpected engineering problems that emerged in scaling up from tiny prototypes to commercial plants slowed progress everywhere.

Private companies showed little interest in commercializing nuclear power in the late fifties. The electricity business was booming, costs were falling and imported oil was cheap. Utility planners saw no need to invest in an expensive and risky new technology. But the U.S. Government was willing to go where the Fortune 500 feared to tread. The United States spent hundreds of millions of dollars on the Power Reactor Demonstration Program, in which large corporations built a half-dozen prototype nuclear power plants, attempting to prove the economic viability of the technology.[7]

As the demonstration plants were completed in the early sixties, the U.S. Atomic Energy Commission and nuclear equipment manufacturers mounted a campaign to convince utilities that nuclear costs could be lowered substantially. The Atomic Energy Commission's *Report to the President* in 1962 concluded that nuclear power was at

9

"the threshold of economic competitiveness" with other electricity sources.[8] Although this claim was made on an exceedingly slim data base, many planners became convinced that nuclear power would soon be a commercial reality. Private utilities were further prompted by increasingly explicit government threats to turn nuclear power over to public agencies such as the Tennessee Valley Authority—as had been done with hydropower in the thirties.[9]

Still, utilities demanded a guarantee that nuclear plants would be cheaper than alternatives. The turning point came in December 1963 when General Electric and the Jersey Central Power & Light Company signed a contract for a "turnkey" nuclear plant that G.E. built at a set price, competitive with the cost of a coal-fired plant. The utility risked little since it simply paid the agreed price when construction was complete and then "turned the key" to begin generating power. A small wave of eight similar agreements followed, launching commercial nuclear power in the United States. Although these plants did not actually produce power for several years, the signed contracts seemed to substantiate manufacturers' claims that the technology was mature.[10]

The next stage came quickly. In 1966 and 1967 utilities ordered 51 more nuclear plants, signing open-ended, "cost-plus" contracts that shifted the burden of any future cost overruns to the utilities and their customers. By the end of 1967 the United States had 28 times as much nuclear power capacity on order as it had in operation. The four U.S. companies selling nuclear reactors competed aggressively for new orders, and utilities rushed to stay at the forefront of the technology. Nuclear power was considered inevitable for meeting future electricity demand, which was doubling every ten years.

Economists Irvin Bupp and Jean-Claude Derian aptly describe this period as a "Great Bandwagon Market" for nuclear power.[11] The resulting euphoria discouraged dispassionate analysis of the state of nuclear technology. Utilities had little understanding of the more demanding engineering that nuclear power plants required, and no economic history existed to assess the vendors' claims. Each additional order was simply taken as evidence of the accuracy of those claims. Bupp and Derian said that, "The rush to nuclear power had become a self-sustaining process." Perhaps self-sustaining, but not sustainable indefinitely without further proof of economic competitiveness.

The apparent commercial success of nuclear power in the United States boosted nuclear power programs around the world. By the early sixties, Great Britain and France had built successful prototype gas-cooled reactors, and Canada was well along in developing its heavy water reactor design. But most analysts had concluded that economical nuclear power was at least several years away in all of these countries. In 1970 an authoritative French report conceded that, "Aside from Great Britain and Canada, the success of nuclear power is the success of American light water reactors . . . which overwhelm all markets where true competition exists."[12] The Soviet Union's nuclear program also lagged well behind that in the United States, with only eight small nuclear plants operating by the late sixties.

Beginning in the mid-sixties, U.S. companies aggressively marketed nuclear technologies in Europe, Japan and some developing nations. The companies were assisted by the U.S. Government's Atoms for Peace program, designed to counter the Soviet Union's successes in courting Third World nations. More than a dozen countries purchased American-designed plants or signed licensing agreements with U.S. companies. Today France, Japan and West Germany, which, along with the United States, play a prominent role in the nuclear power industry, all build nuclear plants based on U.S. designs. Nuclear power was easier to develop in Europe than in the United States, given a strong tradition of government control of the utility industry and the many links between government officials, banks and private corporations. With the rapid growth of electricity demand and the relative scarcity of indigenous energy resources in Europe, few challenged the notion that nuclear power deserved a high priority.[13]

The late sixties and early seventies also marked a great expansion of Third World nuclear power programs. Nuclear power was welcomed as an alternative to imported oil and as a way for developing countries to propel themselves into the twentieth century. Exports of the technology were vigorously promoted by the multinational corporations that dominate the industry and by government agencies such as the U.S. Export-Import Bank. The International Atomic Energy Agency, an arm of the United Nations, was also influential in selling nuclear power in the Third World. Sixteen developing countries, some still relying on fuelwood as their major domestic energy source, had nuclear power programs by the mid-seventies. Argentina, Brazil, India, South Korea and Taiwan are among the countries that pushed hardest. The head of Pakistan's Atomic Energy Commission said, "For many developing countries nuclear power is simply a matter of survival."[14]

By 1973 worldwide nuclear power capacity had risen to 43,000 megawatts, provided by 115 plants. The United States had half the total capacity and Great Britain one-eighth. France and the Soviet Union each had the equivalent of only three 1000-megawatt nuclear plants, and Canada, Japan and West Germany, only two each. But nuclear construction programs were in full swing in a half-dozen countries, and a dozen more programs were planned to begin soon. In the peak growth years of 1971 through 1974, over 200 nuclear power plants were ordered worldwide, approximately doubling the number of planned reactors.[15]

The 1973-74 oil crisis was widely regarded as the final guarantee that nuclear power would be the world's next preeminent energy source. Western political leaders saw nuclear power as the necessary high-technology solution to OPEC's stranglehold on the oil market. The Nixon administration's "Project Independence" aimed for nuclear power to supply half of U.S. electricity by the year 2000. French Prime Minister Jacques Chirac spoke for many when he said in early 1975, "For the immediate future, I mean for the coming ten years, nuclear energy is one of the main answers to our energy needs."[16]

Adding Up The Costs

When the Grand Gulf 1 nuclear power plant was ordered in 1972, the Mississippi Power and Light Company estimated that it would cost about $300 million. In 1983 the plant began generating power several years behind schedule and $2.5 billion over budget. This figure is remarkable not just for its magnitude; it is also about average for the U.S. nuclear industry.

"Sixteen developing countries,
some still relying on fuelwood as their
major domestic energy source, had nuclear power
programs by the mid-seventies."

Nuclear power plants completed in the United States in the next few years will generally cost five to ten times as much as originally projected—overruns of more than $2 billion each. And some projects make that figure look like a bargain. The Limerick 1 plant in Pennsylvania is now budgeted at $3.4 billion, and the Nine Mile Point 2 plant in New York is expected to cost between $4.6 billion and $5.6 billion. Several recently canceled nuclear plants would have cost as much as $8 billion each had they been completed. Even the few "success stories" claimed by the U.S. nuclear industry, such as the Palo Verde plants in Arizona, are over budget and will cost over $2.5 billion each. Nuclear economics is not for the fainthearted. The annual cost overruns alone equal the government budgets of many nations.[17]

13

Thirty years have passed since U.S. nuclear officials said nuclear power would be "too cheap to meter."[18] It was an unfortunate claim that the nuclear industry now wishes had never been made. But these words will be long remembered, for they mark the beginning of a sad history of bold assertions and unsupported analysis that made the actual cost and economic merits of nuclear power extremely uncertain. Even today a full and fair accounting of the economic status of nuclear power is hard to find in any country. Some of the most misleading reports, unfortunately, come from government and industry offices that should have access to the most complete data.

The 650-megawatt Oyster Creek plant that launched the commercial nuclear power industry in 1963 was sold for $64 million, or about $100 per kilowatt of capacity. For Jersey Central Power and Light, the reactor was a bargain source of electricity. For the nuclear industry, Oyster Creek and the eight other "turnkey" nuclear plants that followed were huge "loss leaders," on which the plant manufacturers lost between $800 million and $1 billion. But these projects served their intended role by helping create the first bona fide market for nuclear power plants.[19]

In the late sixties completed nuclear power plants cost between $250 and $300 per kilowatt rather than the $150 per kilowatt predicted when the projects were started.[20] Nuclear industry officials were little concerned since they assumed that nuclear power would soon follow the traditional "learning curve" in which design and construction techniques improve and costs fall. The utilities signaled their confidence by ordering 126 nuclear power plants between 1971 and the end of 1974—enough to increase total U.S. generating capacity in the early seventies by nearly half.

14 By the mid-seventies enough non-turnkey nuclear plants were finished to begin assessing actual nuclear costs. The facts were not encouraging. Studies by Irvin Bupp of the Harvard Business School and William Mooz of the Rand Corporation showed that most nuclear power plants cost substantially more than expected and that costs were rising steadily over time.[21] Although respected analysts made these estimates using standard accounting procedures, the danger warnings were drowned out by the continued optimistic claims of nuclear manufacturers. Industry consultants published studies showing that nuclear power was more economical than any other power source and that cost increases were temporary, caused by inflation and regulatory delays.[22]

The economic case for nuclear power became far more difficult to make as construction cost estimates for virtually every plant under construction climbed steadily during the late seventies. In 1981 economist Charles Komanoff published a thorough assessment of cost trends in the nuclear industry. Using the utilities' own data, but carefully separating out the effects of inflation and interest rates, he concluded that real (inflation-adjusted) construction costs for nuclear plants had risen 142 percent between 1971 and 1978, or 13.5 percent annually. He found that coal plants were also becoming more expensive (largely due to added pollution control equipment) but at a much lower 7.7 percent annual rate.[23]

Because additional plants tend to reveal more technical problems that require more costly solutions, Komanoff projected that by the late eighties nuclear plants would cost at least $1,800 (1982 dollars) per kilowatt to build, or 75 percent more than coal plants completed at the same time. Originally nuclear plants were expected to cost 10 to 30 percent more than coal plants to build, but lower nuclear fuel costs were supposed to make nuclear power less expensive in the long run. A 75 percent construction cost margin, however, makes nuclear power barely economical at best. The nuclear industry vigorously disputed Komanoff's estimates, arguing that statistical analysis of the recent past does not reliably predict future trends.

To the chagrin of the industry, recent data shows that Komanoff's projections were, if anything, conservative. Since the mid-seventies, cost estimates for individual nuclear plants have risen 20 percent annually. Costs, therefore, doubled every four years, rising faster than those for gasoline, housing or almost anything else. Nuclear plants completed in the mid-eighties will cost an average of almost $2,000 (1982 dollars) per kilowatt to build (interest costs not included), twice as much as coal plants. (See Figure 1.) And because of the high

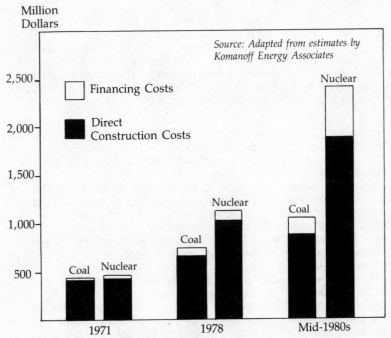

Figure 1: Estimated Average U.S. Construction Costs for 1,000-Megawatt Coal and Nuclear Power Plants by Year of Completion (1982 dollars)

costs and long contruction times, financing charges for a nuclear plant are now three times those for a coal plant and add $500 (1982 dollars) per kilowatt to the average construction bill.[24]

16 Operating costs for nuclear power plants, once expected to be negligible, have become substantial. A 1982 study by economists with the Energy Systems Research Group found that operation and maintenance (O&M) costs rose during the seventies at an average annual rate of 18 percent.[25] By the early eighties, the average nuclear plant cost more than $30 million a year to operate (excluding fuel costs and major capital additions), enough to contribute 20 percent to the cost of nuclear power. Further O&M cost increases appear likely, particularly as plants age and systems deteriorate. Generic technical problems recently discovered in some nuclear plant designs, such as leaky steam generators and brittle reactor vessels, could result in repair bills of hundreds of millions of dollars. Nuclear fuel costs have risen at a much slower rate. They contribute only about 10 percent to the cost of nuclear power and are one of the few factors in the economic equation not giving nightmares to utility executives.[26]

U.S. nuclear power plants have also been hurt by erratic operating schedules. Plants have operated on average at less than 60 percent of their rated capacity in recent years rather than at 75 to 80 percent of rated capacity as originally expected.[27] At fault are a range of technical problems that require operation at partial capacity as well as frequent shutdowns for repairs. Two-thirds of the cost of nuclear electricity comes from construction costs and interest that must be paid regardless of whether the plant is operating, and the Energy Systems Research Group estimates that a drop in capacity factor of 20 percentage points increases the cost of power by 30 percent. Coal plants have also run at about 60 percent of rated capacity, largely due to low power demand and resulting intentional cutbacks. But only a third of coal generation costs are capital costs, so the economic penalty is not nearly as great. Most of today's nuclear power plants are relatively new, and researchers are concerned that as plants age, deteriorating equipment may reduce capacity factors further. Salt water cooled reactors are particularly troublesome because they apparently suffer a significant decline in capacity factor as early as the seventh year of operation, presumably due to corrosion.[28]

"In the nuclear business,
the line between serious analysis
and industry propaganda is frequently blurred."

Industry and government studies have been slow to recognize the declining economic competitiveness of nuclear power. Cost estimates for plants under construction based on traditional engineering assessments continue to miss the mark widely and are adjusted upward by hundreds of millions of dollars each year. Many industrywide studies, failing to distinguish between real cost trends and inflation, simply assume that all increases are caused by inflation and high interest rates. Even the real cost of currently operating nuclear plants is frequently misstated by relying on cumbersome accounting methods and failing to note important trends over time. Since nuclear plants typically take eight to twelve years to build, during which inflation is constantly lowering the real value of money spent, figuring the real (inflation-adjusted) value of each year's work is laborious but essential. Projections of future costs are often even further from the mark since they assume that steeply rising cost curves will soon flatten out. In the nuclear business, the line between serious analysis and industry propaganda is frequently blurred.[29]

17

Even government and industry officials are now much less bullish on the economics of nuclear power. In industry boardrooms and at regulatory hearings, cost overruns are frequently cited as a major problem confronting nuclear power. Lewis Perl, a utility industry consultant who bears responsibility for many reports extolling the economics of nuclear power, now says that, "Continued escalation in capital costs and operating costs for even a couple more years would wipe out the nuclear advantage (over coal)."[30] Though Perl's timing is off, his conclusion is essentially right. On the other hand, a 1982 U.S. Department of Energy (DOE) report concluded that for nuclear and coal plants completed in 1995, total generating costs would be about even, at between 4¢ and 6¢ (1980 dollars) per kilowatt-hour, depending on the region of the country.[31] Though a new admission for DOE, the study is still severely biased in favor of nuclear power. It understates the real cost of nuclear plants now being completed by at least 20 percent and assumes without foundation that construction cost increases will slow drastically in the next few years.

Careful analysis of utility industry data for the 30-odd U.S. nuclear plants scheduled for completion in the mid-eighties shows that they will generate electricity at an average lifetime generating cost of between 10¢ and 12¢ per kilowatt-hour (1982 dollars). This is more than 65 percent above the cost of new coal-fired power and 25 percent higher than new oil-fired power, even assuming substantial fossil fuel price increases. (See Figure 2.)[32] If all the electricity used by Americans cost as much as this nuclear electricity will, the nation's utility bills would rise about 130 percent.[33] As a source of heat, electricity from new nuclear plants at today's delivered cost compares with oil priced at $240 per barrel.[34]

Enough data exists to show conclusively that new nuclear power plants are not cost-effective in the United States compared to new coal

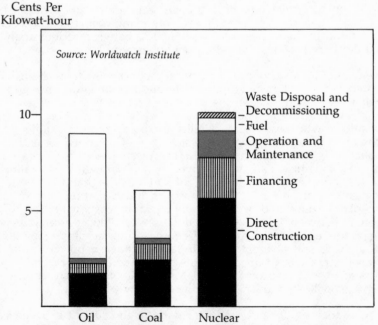

Cents Per
Kilowatt-hour

Source: Worldwatch Institute

Waste Disposal and
Decommissioning
Fuel
Operation and
Maintenance

Financing

Direct
Construction

Oil   Coal   Nuclear

**Figure 2: Estimated Average Lifetime Generating Costs
For U.S. Power Plants Completed In The Mid-Eighties (1982 dollars)**

plants. Even if all the unique safety and health dangers of nuclear power were removed, a U.S. utility planner choosing between a coal or nuclear power plant solely on the basis of economics would have to select coal. Compared with energy efficiency improvements, nuclear power looks even less economically attractive (a comparison that is assessed in the last section of this paper). In addition, nuclear power carries financial risks that that have struck terror in the hearts of many utility executives. S. David Freeman, a director of the Tennessee Valley Authority, which once had the largest nuclear construction program in the United States, concluded in 1982 that, "The cost of nuclear power isn't just high, it's unpredictable. No sane capitalist is going to build something for which he can't derive a cost/benefit ratio because the cost is unknowable."[35]

Outside the United States, the economics of nuclear power is much harder to calculate. In most countries the relatively few operating plants have produced only a slim data base, and few nations release cost figures for individual nuclear plants. As in the United States, companies and government agencies strongly committed to nuclear power selectively release data and sometimes provide biased interpretation of figures they do release. Outside analysts often have insufficient data to scrutinize official claims. Nonetheless, important information is emerging from several key countries.

In Great Britain, the government's nuclear program is at a turning point. The country's advanced gas-cooled plants have had poor operating records, and the Atomic Energy Authority and government-owned utility, the Central Electricity Generating Board (CEGB), have proposed building a new generation of light water nuclear plants based on the American Westinghouse design. The Sizewell Inquiry, a semi-judicial proceeding convened in 1983, is assessing the proposal and will recommend to the government in 1984 whether a light water plant should be built. Already the longest hearing of its kind in British history, the Sizewell Inquiry has become an unprecedented, wide-ranging assessment of nuclear power's economic status in Britain. To the surprise of many, safety and environmental issues have been pushed into the background.[36]

The government has spent several months presenting a detailed case for additional nuclear plants. One of the most telling critiques comes from Gordon Mackerron of the University of Sussex, who concluded in a 1982 report that CEGB estimates for plants already built in Great Britain favored nuclear power by failing to calculate the full value of past capital investments. The CEGB, Mackerron found, had not distinguished clearly between current and constant dollar costs. Regarding the CEGB's future calculations, the government's own Monopolies Commission faulted the utility for consistently using "optimistic" rather than "mid-range" assumptions. Both Gordon Mackerron and J.W. Jeffery, a retired professor at the University of London, have conducted thorough economic assessments of British nuclear plants in recent years. Mackerron concludes that coal and nuclear generating costs in Great Britain are virtually even, with coal power's higher fuel costs largely offset by the much higher capital cost of nuclear power. Jeffery contends that nuclear power is considerably more expensive than coal-fired power.[37]

Although vigorously disputing these figures at first, the CEGB in 1983 had to recant many of its earlier economic claims for British nuclear plants. The latest CEGB figures show that the country's more recent gas-cooled plants cost twice as much to build as coal-fired plants, yielding slightly higher total generating costs. Yet the CEGB continues to press for new light water plants in Great Britain, despite the disappointing U.S. experience with that technology. The CEGB will be challenged by a growing number of analysts who agree with J.W. Jeffery's contention that, "Nuclear power has not been economic, is not economic and is likely to get more uneconomic in the future." Even the British energy establishment believes that the government case has not held up well so far, but the outcome is difficult to predict because political considerations will likely play a major role.[38]

West Germany has a larger and more successful nuclear power program than does Great Britain, but it has suffered from major cost overruns nonetheless. Official figures compiled by Rheinisch-Westfälisches Elektrizitätswerk (RWE), the country's dominant investor-owned utility, show direct nuclear construction costs rising sixfold between 1969 and 1982 while coal plant construction costs went up less than fourfold. The utility concluded that nuclear costs, after allowing for the effects of inflation, had risen at an annual rate of 9 percent while coal costs had risen 4.6 percent annually. The RWE figures indicate that nuclear plants completed in 1985 are likely to cost

150 percent more than coal-fired plants. Another set of official projections made in 1982 for plants begun in that year (for completion in 1993) show nuclear capital costs of DM 5000 ($1800) per kilowatt in current dollars compared to DM 2500 ($900) per kilowatt for a coal plant.[39]

Coal prices are relatively high in West Germany, providing some basis for the government's claim that nuclear power still has a lifetime generating cost advantage over coal-fired power. But nuclear power is unlikely to overcome a capital cost margin as large as the one officials now admit to. Critics charge that West German nuclear planners consistently underestimate the cost of nuclear projects and use accounting methods that do not measure the full cost of nuclear electricity generation. A major study by Jürgen Franke and Dieter Viefhues of the Institut Freiburg concluded in 1983 that due to rapidly escalating construction costs and interest rates, nuclear electricity from plants begun today will cost at least 60 percent more than coal-fired power. According to Franke and Viefhues, even under the most optimistic assumptions, a case for ordering additional nuclear plants in West Germany no longer exists.[40]

France is a key country in international comparisons of nuclear economics. With perhaps the only nuclear construction program running at near full capacity in recent years, France has an international reputation for efficiency and speed. Though U.S. nuclear plants take on average almost ten years to build, French plants average less than six years. Official French figures published in 1982 show real capital costs rising from FF 2450 ($350-$500) per kilowatt in 1974 to FF 3500 ($500-$700) per kilowatt in 1981—all expressed in 1981 francs—a relatively modest 43 percent increase. This works out to an annual rate of increase of 5 percent, one-third the rate in the American nuclear industry and one-half the West German rate. The figure is corroborated by a 3-5 percent annual real rate of increase reported to Komanoff by Électricité de France, the country's national utility, in 1981. French planners maintain that nuclear plants cost just 17 percent more to build than coal plants and that overall, nuclear power is 20-40 percent cheaper than coal-fired power.[41]

The meager cost data released by French authorities makes the veracity of the official numbers hard to prove. Most of the figures released are aggregates compiled by planners with a vested interest in their program. Data for individual plants is not available, so figures cannot be confirmed or correlated with relevant variables. Official accounting techniques are not described and could easily hide major subsidies for the nuclear program.[42]

At least relative to other countries, however, the French nuclear program has been an economic success. The margin may not be as large as official figures indicate, but nuclear power in France does appear to be significantly less expensive than coal-fired power. Capacity factors and operating costs for French plants, however, have suffered from poor performance since 1982, which will likely raise costs. Only more time and experience will tell how economical France's ambitious nuclear program really is.

The limited information available for other nations also shows substantial cost increases during the past decade. In Japan average real construction costs have gone from 100,000 yen ($425) per kilowatt in the early seventies to 280,000 yen ($1,200) per kilowatt in the early eighties (all in 1982 yen), according to utility industry sources. Japanese nuclear plants now cost 140 percent more than coal plants to build. In the Soviet Union the latest Five-Year Plan reports that nuclear plants are 80 to 100 percent more expensive to build than coal plants. In Sweden utility industry figures show that the real cost of nuclear projects has risen at a 7.5 percent annual rate, and generating costs for the latest Swedish reactors come to between 2.9¢ and 4.2¢ per kilowatt-hour.[43]

In Canada, the country's CANDU reactors have some of the best operating records among nuclear plants worldwide. But data released by Ontario Hydro, the builder of Canada's CANDU nuclear plants, shows that construction costs rose from $400 per kilowatt in 1972 to $1,700 per kilowatt in the early eighties, or a real rate of increase of 6 percent after inflation. Critics of Canada's nuclear program argue that new nuclear plants will generate power that is several times as expensive as hydropower now being harnessed. In India the government now admits that nuclear power is much more expensive than coal-fired electricity, but justifies its large nuclear program in terms of national prestige and technological leadership.[44]

> "In the Soviet Union
> the latest Five-Year Plan reports
> that nuclear plants are 80 to 100 percent more expensive
> to build than coal plants."

Table 2: Annual Real Rates of Increase of Nuclear Construction Costs Since The Early Seventies In Selected Countries

Country	Installed Nuclear Capacity, 1983	Annual Cost Increase
	(1,000 megawatts)	(percent)
United States	60	13
France	22	5
Japan	17	11
West Germany	10	9
Sweden	7	8
Canada	7	6

Source: Worldwatch Institute.

Comparing nuclear economics internationally in strictly quantitative terms is a hopeless endeavor. Not only is comprehensive and reliable data scarce, but constant variations in inflation, exchange rates and fuel costs make common standards difficult to apply. Enough data is available, however, to show that cost overruns have been most severe in the United States, West Germany and Great Britain. But cost increases above inflation have been near-universal—even in such "model" nuclear countries as France and Japan. (See Table 2.) These trends have badly hurt nuclear power's economic standing compared to its most direct competitor—coal-fired power. Perhaps most disturbing from a long-term view is that the economics of nuclear power seems to worsen over time in most countries. Many are poised to repeat the disappointing experience with nuclear power in the United States.

Roots of the Crisis: A Full Accounting?

Explanations for the rising cost of nuclear power provoke enormous disagreement. The nuclear manufacturers generally blame their woes on excessive government regulation or a harsh economic climate, while nuclear critics blame inept management or a flawed technology. All of these factors and several others play a role, but safety is almost certainly the single most important issue in understanding cost trends in the nuclear industry. Nuclear proponents and critics agree that nuclear plants must be safe to be a viable energy source, and the measures taken to improve safety account for a large share of rising costs. From nuclear power's earliest days the cost of particular safeguards has stirred controversy. Many proposed regulations were not issued because of their potential economic impact, according to a study by Daniel Ford of the Union of Concerned Scientists.[45]

The designers, builders and regulators of nuclear plants in the late fifties and early sixties gradually discovered the complexity of the engineering needed to ensure the safety of nuclear power. The dozens of interlocking systems that had to work in synchrony were often unlike any that had been built before. Nuclear plants pushed many materials and engineering standards beyond their limits, while the scale of the projects caused unprecedented management difficulties. The broad "general design criteria" issued by government regulators were about as helpful as a quick sketch would be to a company building a skyscraper. Regulators began issuing more specific requirements almost immediately and plant builders had to introduce many innovations of their own.[46]

Much of the cost overruns for nuclear plants planned in the sixties can be attributed to the unrealistically low bids made by manufacturers trying to sell their product to the utilities. Engineers found serious design flaws in the early plants that required costly correction. Regulators, both in the United States and Europe, assumed that nuclear power was a mature technology and so dealt with these various problems individually as they arose. Overall plant design was never thoroughly reassessed.

Stabilizing plant design was further complicated by efforts to increase the size of the plants. Size became a major selling point for the nuclear companies since economies of scale were expected to lower the cost per kilowatt. The manufacturers abandoned their usual conservative approach to scaling up new technologies, and plants ordered in the United States increased from an average of 300 megawatts in 1962 to 700 megawatts in 1965 and 1,150 megawatts in 1972.[47] By the late sixties nuclear plants under construction were six times

"Engineers found serious design flaws
in the early plants that required
costly correction."

larger than any then in operation. West German officials report that the rapid scaling up of their nuclear plants resulted in many technical problems and cost overruns.[48]

The rapidly increasing size of nuclear power plants affected many aspects of plant design. Larger nuclear cores contain more radioactive fission products and have a greater power density, increasing the danger in the event of an accident. The potential for a plant meltdown steadily grew as plant size increased. Beginning in the early sixties containment structures became essential to prevent the release of radioactive materials. Emergency core-cooling systems, which remove heat from the core in the event of a breakdown, were introduced, enlarged and provided with backups. The response time of the various safety systems had to be shortened and each became vastly more complicated.[49]

25

By 1970, when the first nuclear plant with a capacity over 600 megawatts began operating, more than 50 plants of similar or greater size had been ordered. Actual experience with these large, new plants produced some unpleasant surprises. Pumps, valves and electrical systems broke down, fires erupted, radioactive water-leaks contaminated equipment and workers, and essential safety systems were occasionally shut down by accident. Similar problems might have plagued a new automated automobile factory or cement plant, but at nuclear plants they raised grave safety concerns.

Earthquake resistance typifies the problems encountered. Though engineers first considered earthquake damage when nuclear plants were proposed in California in the mid-sixties, they soon realized that earthquakes could disable a plant's safety systems in most regions of the world. New seismic standards had to be developed and then gradually changed over time. Blueprints for plants often had to be reworked as standards changed. Most disruptive were new standards imposed on plants already under construction. As a result, many of today's nuclear plants are cluttered with oddly-positioned support structures, making it hard for workers to move about. At the Diablo Canyon plant in California, built near a major offshore fault, seismic improvements have led to cost overruns of hundreds of millions of dollars. Plant operation has been delayed several years simply to verify the adequacy of the plant's seismic design.[50]

Safety-related nuclear components, whether cooling systems, electrical wiring or containment structures, must have several backup systems. This philosophy of redundant design has even extended to the control room, which in some cases has a complete backup should the first become disabled. Today most nuclear plants have at least three diesel generators with a combined capacity of over 100 megawatts. The generators supply power to the plant's safety systems during an emergency in which the plant shuts down and outside power is cut off. In many cases generators have been added after the plant is completed, requiring a new building to house them.

Simply ensuring that all nuclear power plant systems meet required standards has become extremely complicated. Donald Brand, a vice-president of the Pacific Gas and Electric Company in California, describing the procedures for safety-related wiring in the Diablo Canyon plant, said, "For each circuit we can tell you what kind of wire was used, the names of the installing crew, the reel from which it came, the manufacturing test and production history. The tension on the wire when it is pulled is recorded and the tensioning device is calibrated on a periodic basis."[51] In West Germany a similar degree of documentation is required and has reportedly added significantly to costs. Operating experience, including faulty welds, stuck valves and mixed-up blueprints, has provided little reason for easing quality assurance standards.[52]

Figures for the past decade show that the amount of concrete, piping and cable used in an average nuclear plant has more than doubled and that labor requirements have more than tripled.[53] Not all of the costs can be explained so easily, however. The changes needed to make nuclear plants safer affect not only discrete components but complex, interrelated systems. Often one change results in another, and so on. A study by the Atomic Industrial Forum in the U.S. noted that, "Attempts have been made on numerous occasions to pinpoint the full impact of regulatory changes on a nuclear project, and in each case it was found that the total impact was inevitably larger than the sum of the parts."[54]

Economist Charles Komanoff observed in his cost-trends study that, "Reactors were increasingly built in an 'environment of constant change' that precluded control or even estimation of costs and spurred endemic inefficiency in design and construction."[55] Many procedures were performed poorly by inexperienced workers, some had to be undone in order to allow for changes in other components, and constructicn crews often sat idle while waiting for parts to arrive or for supervisors to solve a difficult problem. Changes are made more complicated in the United States by literally scores of unique power plant designs, each of which must be individually evaluated and modified. Chronic inefficiency has become a trademark of many nuclear industries.[56]

The near-meltdown at the Three Mile Island nuclear plant in 1979 generated a new wave of changes in plant design and construction, even outside the United States. The accident revealed critical weaknesses in systems assumed to be sound. The pioneering nuclear physicist Alvin Weinberg reflected the general philosophy that emerged from the Three Mile Island accident when he said, "For nuclear energy to grow in usefulness, the accident probability per reactor will simply have to diminish."[57] Both industry officials and regulators looked more critically at plant design and found a wide range of generic technical problems that would have to be corrected at all plants to ensure adequate safety. Even today the changes continue, and most operating nuclear plants in the United States resemble construction sites. Marc Budaj, an engineer at New Jersey's Oyster Creek reactor, the first commercial plant in the United States, expressed the frustration of many in the nuclear industry in the early eighties when he said, "When they are decommissioning this power plant, and pouring concrete in the reactor vessel, there'll still be some engineers out there installing field changes."[58]

One reason changes are so expensive is that many projects are mismanaged. The large engineering firms that direct nuclear projects in many countries sign "cost-plus" contracts with the utilities. (Fluid plant design and component costs make it virtually impossible to set a firm price and hold the builder to it.) Under the cost-plus system, the lead company and its subcontractors have little incentive to minimize costs. In fact, incentives are strong to stretch out construction and raise the total bill since profits are usually calculated as a fixed percentage of the project's cost. Utilities in turn pass all costs along to their customers, regulators permitting. Even those utilities that do rigorously attempt to control costs often lack the staff to ride herd on the project. This system has made nuclear power highly profitable for many of the engineering firms that build nuclear plants, though not for the major vendors.[59]

France has largely avoided the "environment of constant change" that characterizes most of the world's nuclear power programs. The French program, begun only in the early seventies, is based on an American design that had been tested for a decade. As a result, France avoided the costly and time-consuming task of designing a nuclear plant from scratch. French planners paved new ground, however, by concentrating early on two standardized plant designs—one of 900 megawatts and the second of 1,300 megawatts. This allowed the traditional learning process to unfold and helps account for the apparently slower rate of cost escalation in France.[60]

Costs have also been kept in check by consolidating responsibility for building all the country's nuclear power plants under one agency, Electricité de France (EDF). The utility both accumulates considerable experience and, since it pays for the plants, has a direct incentive to keep them within budget. The United States, in contrast, has dozens of utilities with nuclear projects, and most, because they usually build just one or two, have little expertise. In France, EDF is an adjunct of the national government and has much broader authority than comparable agencies in most countries. French regulators and industry officials avoid confrontation, and many issues are settled across a lunch table, rather than in a hearing room. Citizens groups or local governments opposing a particular project on economic, safety or environmental grounds have little opportunity to intervene in the decision-making process.

The nuclear industry argues strenuously that inept regulation is at the root of the cost increases that plague it in most countries. The growth of regulation has indeed had an impact on cost. Some ad hoc requirements have added little to plant safety, and regulators have reversed themselves frequently. But blaming nuclear cost overruns on regulators alone is like killing the messenger who carries bad news.

Regulatory standards are essential for correcting inadequate technologies that frequently break down and industries that are often paragons of inefficiency. As former Nuclear Regulatory Commissioner

> "France's unprecedented degree
> of nuclear standardization has made it possible
> to have politically acceptable safety standards
> without constantly altering plant designs."

Peter Bradford has said, many of the industry's problems "lie in an omnivorous dream of growth that swept aside sensible regulation, sensible planning and sensible government attention to the side effects." Evidence grows of fundamental problems in many aspects of current plant design that will need further upgrading in order to prevent accidents. S. David Freeman said, "We ought to realize that with nuclear power, we are still experimenting. . . We stopped the research and development effort much too soon." Reduced regulation without fundamental changes in nuclear technology and management could make nuclear plants less safe, but not necessarily less expensive.[61]

There are risks even when nuclear power is "well-managed." France's unprecedented degree of nuclear standardization has made it possible to have politically acceptable safety standards without constantly altering plant designs. But France has only a few years of operating experience with its large nuclear plants, and the performance and safety levels that officials claim remain to be proved. The standardized design adopted by the French also poses an inherent risk, since a generic technical problem may be discovered that would plague most of the country's reactors. Whether this gamble succeeds will not be known for several years, and already French Atomic Energy Agency officials have privately warned that plant safety designs may be inadequate.[62] Other nations hoping to copy the French model must also decide whether to entrust energy policy to an agency authorized to spend billions of dollars in a single-minded pursuit of nuclear power.

Important uncounted costs may further tip the economic scales against nuclear power. Disposal of nuclear wastes and decommissioning old nuclear plants are important factors in the overall equation, and yet neither has been resolved or even adequately researched in any country. Nuclear wastes continue to pile up in temporary storage, and most nuclear plant operators do not have procedures for permanently shutting down plants after their presumed 30-year life span is over. How much these two problems will eventually add to the cost of nuclear power is highly uncertain.

Radioactive wastes are an inevitable by-product of nuclear power generation. From uranium mining to fuel fabrication and plant operation, many waste products with varying levels of radioactivity must be disposed of properly. Particularly troublesome are the highly radioactive spent fuel assemblies removed periodically from operating nuclear plants, which must be kept from human exposure for hundreds or thousands of years. Between 15,000 and 20,000 tons of these materials have been produced in nuclear power plants worldwide, most of it still stored in temporary facilities at reactor sites.[63]

Options for long-term disposal include dumping wastes in Antarctica or launching them into space, but for safety and health reasons, attention has focused on burial in stable geological formations. West Germany leads in developing such disposal sites—in natural salt deposits—but most countries are still only investigating the possibilities. High-level wastes must be prevented from leaking into ground water, and from there to the larger biosphere. Many geologists doubt that long-term guarantees will ever be possible. The United States, which has the most high-level radioactive wastes, did not enact a detailed waste disposal law until 1982. The law requires the Department of Energy (DOE) to develop a working plan for waste disposal by 1990. DOE is apparently already behind schedule, and major technical uncertainties and political battles are sure to frustrate efforts to meet the Congressionally mandated target.[64]

Also of concern are uranium mining wastes and low-level wastes, which include a wide variety of materials that have been exposed to radiation—even workers' clothes. Although not as hazardous as high-level wastes, low-level wastes are so abundant that they pose daunting disposal problems. According to a U.S. Government estimate made in the mid-seventies, the United States might produce a billion cubic feet of such wastes by the end of the century, enough to cover a four-lane coast-to-coast highway a foot deep. Much of this material is currently buried in shallow trenches or dumped at sea, but many scientists argue that this practice, if continued indefinitely, will cause ecological and health damage. Some of the low-level wastes last for decades and would eventually enter the food chain.[65]

No thorough accounting of the cost of dealing effectively with the world's nuclear waste disposal problems exists. Many utilities and governments do set aside some limited funds for this purpose, however. In the United States, utilities must cover the cost of waste

"Critics of nuclear power argue
that the country has built 'a house with no toilets'
and that Japan should stop building plants
until disposal problems have been solved."

disposal by paying the government $1 for every 1,000 kilowatt-hours generated. But the many leaks and false starts encountered in early waste disposal efforts portend still higher costs, adding an estimated 5-10 percent to the total cost of nuclear power.[66]

The significance of the waste disposal issue goes far beyond these uncertain figures. Since 1976 California has banned construction of new nuclear power plants because unresolved waste disposal problems might limit a plant's useful life and ruin its economic viability. In 1983 that law was upheld by the U.S. Supreme Court on the grounds that states have the right to regulate economic aspects of nuclear power. Japan, crowded and prone to earthquakes, has a particularly acute waste disposal problem. Critics of nuclear power argue that the country has built "a house with no toilets" and that Japan should stop building plants until disposal problems have been solved.[67]

The decommissioning of old nuclear power plants presents similar economic worries. The term "decommissioning" is a misnomer since it implies a routine shutdown procedure similar to abandoning an old coal mine. But nuclear plants that have been operating for decades have many parts that are radioactive and must be kept from the biosphere for centuries. One approach is called "entombment"— sealing a plant with reinforced concrete and providing guards for an indefinite period. But entombment, though possibly economical, poses unacceptable long-term environmental problems, particularly since some materials would remain radioactive for as long as 100,000 years, long past the useful life of concrete. Ensuring the integrity of human institutions to provide centuries of guard duty is also problematic. Nuclear industry officials cringe at the notion of hundreds of nuclear "tombs" around the world serving as a reminder of the long-term hazards of nuclear power.[68]

The more likely approach to decommissioning is dismantling each nuclear plant piece by piece, and transporting radioactive materials to suitable waste sites. The technical difficulties involved are considerable. Because of the high levels of radiation that would be encountered, elaborate safeguards must be used to limit human exposure. Some parts of the reactor would have to be dismantled underwater in special pools using remote-control torches. Other procedures would have to be done in many shifts to limit the radiation received by individual workers to acceptable levels.

32 Cost estimates for dismantling a 1000-megawatt nuclear plant range from $50 million to over $1 billion (1982 dollars). The largest plant yet dismantled was the tiny 22-megawatt Elk River plant in Minnesota. The procedure required two years and $6 million, but provided few lessons for dismantling plants fifty times as large and hundreds of times more radioactive. Yet the low costs frequently cited by the nuclear industry are based on extrapolation of the Elk River experience. More revealing is the Shippingport plant, scheduled for decommissioning in the mid- eighties at a cost of $60 million to $70 million, according to a contract signed in late 1983. The difficulties that may be involved in decommissioning are illustrated by the cleanup of the disabled Three Mile Island plant, which has encountered a wide range of unanticipated problems and will cost well over $1 billion.[69]

Utilities in most countries are required to earmark funds for decommissioning nuclear plants. West German planners set aside decommissioning funds equal to 17 percent of the cost of building a plant. In the United States, the benchmark figure required in most states is 10 percent, matching estimates made in government studies. (Some researchers believe that the final cost could be 50 percent or more of construction costs.) This money, however, is generally a "shadow account," since it is not separated from the rest of a utility's assets. Only six U.S. states in 1983 require that the funds be held in separate reserve accounts. In the United States, 51 nuclear plants are scheduled for decommissioning in the decade from 2003 to 2012, which could be a major burden for utilities even if the lower cost estimates prove accurate.[70]

In no other industries are shutdown costs a significant fraction of initial capital costs. Yet nuclear power development has continued without a full assessment of decommissioning costs or efforts to secure sufficient funds, another sign of nuclear power's protection from market forces. A joint government-utility effort to dismantle a large nuclear plant is needed so that a price tag can be placed on decommissioning and reasonable set-aside requirements be implemented. Utilities would be wise to consider these figures when deciding whether to build a nuclear plant. Leaving these questions unanswered is not only dangerous to society but violates fundamental business principles. No clearheaded capitalist will proceed with nuclear development as long as waste disposal and decommissioning remain unresolved.

Financial Meltdown in the United States

The country that led the way into the age of nuclear power may very well lead the way out. The first signs of trouble for the U.S. nuclear industry came in the mid-seventies. Eleven nuclear projects were canceled in 1975 and another 32 from 1976 through 1979. During this period only 13 nuclear plants were ordered. Many energy analysts argued that this was a mid-course correction, a downward blip in nuclear power's healthy future. They were wrong. The early eighties have witnessed a massive trimming of nuclear power programs by most of the country's utilities. Sixteen plants were canceled in 1980, the year after the Three Mile Island accident; six were canceled in 1981; and a record 18 in 1982.[71]

A total of 87 nuclear plants were eliminated in the United States between 1975 and November 1983, with a net loss in future generating capacity of 83,000 megawatts. (See Figure 3.) The Tennessee Valley Authority eliminated 12 of the 17 nuclear plants it planned to build. The Public Service Electric and Gas Company of New Jersey canceled five of eight. The Duke Power Company canceled six of 13. Total cancellations represent 30 percent more nuclear capacity than the United States currently has operating, enough to meet the total electricity needs of any country except the Soviet Union and the United States. Meanwhile, U.S. commitments to coal plants had a net increase of 58,000 megawatts.[72]

Nuclear recession in the United States runs deep: only two nuclear plants ordered in the last nine years have not been subsequently canceled. (No work has been done on these two "phantom" plants and they are unlikely ever to be completed.) The first cancellations cost little since ground had not yet been broken for these plants. But in the last several years plants as much as 10-20 percent complete have been scrapped. In 1982 alone, plants on which $5.7 billion had been spent were canceled, bringing the total bill for discontinued plants to $10 billion. Only a rapidly shrinking list of plants not at least half built (and therefore costly to cancel) can slow the cancellations.[73]

Behind the cancellations lie not only massive cost overruns but fundamental changes in the economic condition of the U.S. utility industry. High inflation and interest rates have made it more difficult to finance long-term, capital-intensive projects. Electricity demand growth has fallen from 7 percent per year a decade ago to between 1 percent and 3 percent today, greatly reducing the need for additional power plants. The persistent failure of utilities to forecast demand correctly

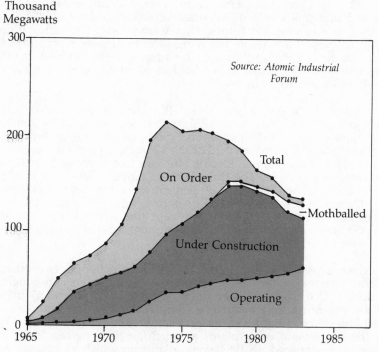

Figure 3: U.S. Commitment to Nuclear Power, 1965–83

and to alter plans soon after trends shifted has further hurt the financial condition of utilities. The Edison Electric Institute, which represents the U.S. utility industry, has been forced to lower its long-term electricity demand projections in each of its last nine annual forecasts. U.S. Department of Energy forecasters have been no more accurate, and their bullish 1983 long-term projection appears well out of line with current trends.[74]

Nuclear projects reveal inherent weaknesses in the curious blend of free market economics and bureaucratic decision making that has severely tested U.S. energy policy. Between power generation and the consumer stand a maze of monopolistic companies, various layers of government regulation and special tax provisions that distort the decision-making process. It is a "free market" system that Adam Smith would hardly recognize and that few policymakers really understand.

Most utilities in the United States are investor-owned and obtain capital mainly by selling electricity, issuing stock to investors and borrowing on the capital markets. State regulators determine rates, usually based on a utility's investment in generating plants and other equipment. Throughout the fifties and sixties, utility stocks were considered safe, "blue chip" investments, often purchased by large institutions and by small investors looking for a haven for their savings. Plant costs fell during this period, and utilities became complacent in their regulated, risk-free environment.

Since the mid-seventies, however, nuclear projects have drained the capital budgets of many utilities. Annual investment in nuclear construction rose from $2 billion in 1970 to $19 billion in 1982, a fourfold increase after discounting for inflation. (See Figure 4.) Though nuclear plants claimed only one-third of utilities' expenditures for new plants in 1970, they took two-thirds by 1983. Spending on nuclear construction in 1983 is more than one-fourth the annual investment in new plant and equipment of the U.S. manufacturing sector and over three times that of the automobile industry.[75]

As capital outlays soared and electricity demand stagnated, the utilities' financial condition deteriorated. The proportion of expenditures that could be met using cash on hand fell, causing a rapid increase in borrowing and stock issuance just when interest rates were high and stock prices low. One measure of financial health is the ratio of market value to book value of a utility's assets. This figure stood at between 1.8 and 2.5 in the sixties but has gradually fallen to between 0.7 and 1.0 since 1974. (See Figure 5.)[76]

Wall Street has signaled utilities to trim nuclear power programs. Leonard Hyman of the Merrill Lynch Company said in 1981 that, "The market requires and is getting a moderately higher rate of return

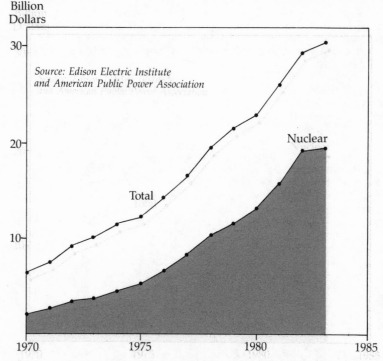

Figure 4: U.S. Utilities' Expenditures for New Generating Plants, 1970–83

"Many financial advisors now warn investors to avoid utilities with nuclear projects."

from investments in utilities that are constructing nuclear power plants." Utilities with nuclear construction programs have lower stock prices and bond ratings on average than utilities that do not.[77] Many financial advisors now warn investors to avoid utilities with nuclear projects. The Three Mile Island accident and its billion-dollar-plus bill for cleanup costs alone has forced the investment community to rethink the financial risk equation. Many believe that the utility industry as a whole is badly underinsured for such an accident. Robert Barrett, a vice-president at Paine, Webber, Jackson & Curtis, calls nuclear power "a potential time bomb that could push a company to the brink of bankruptcy overnight."[78]

37

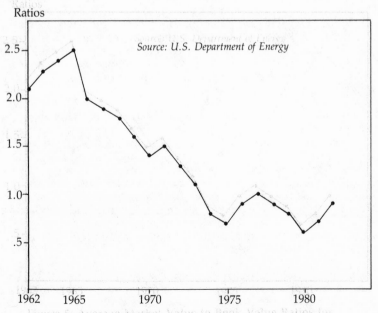

Figure 5: Average Market Value to Book Value Ratios for
U.S. Investor-Owned Utilities, 1962–82

Financial constraints have driven utilities with ongoing nuclear programs to great lengths to raise capital.[79] Borrowing short-term funds at usurious interest rates and "creative financing" are common. The Consumers Power Company of Michigan, builder of the troubled Midland nuclear plant, has issued commercial paper against the utility's oil, gas and coal inventories, sold and leased back the company's headquarters building, and borrowed heavily on the Eurodollar markets.[80] When massive emergency transfusions become commonplace, a patient is usually in deep trouble. The fortunate utilities are those that have cut their losses and gotten out early.

Financial troubles in the utility industry often lead to higher rates for customers. U.S. electricity rates have more than tripled since 1973 after near stability during the previous decade. Higher fuel prices caused much of the increase, but rising nuclear construction costs have become increasingly important. Ribbon-cutting ceremonies for nuclear facilities will soon inaugurate a brave new world of 30-50 percent higher electric bills, a phenomenon described by some as "rate shock." In New England the twin Seabrook plants could cause rates to more than double. Many utility commissions are now torn between keeping electricity affordable and providing utilities with enough revenue to preserve their financial health.[81]

Despite these rate hikes, the utility industry argues that regulators have not permitted enough increases to let it spend as much capital on new plants as needed. This claim is questionable considering the large tax incentives for capital investment and the substantial overcapacity that many utilities have for the foreseeable future. In fact, when rate commissions prevented some utilities from charging consumers for construction work in progress, unneeded plants were canceled that would have cost consumers billions. Had utilities been able to bill customers immediately for virtually any investment, the day of market reckoning for nuclear power would have come much later and been more costly.[82]

One utility that particularly concerns state regulators is the Long Island Lighting Company (Lilco), builder of the 820-megawatt Shoreham nuclear plant in New York. Ordered in 1967, the plant is now scheduled to be completed in 1984 at a cost of $3.4 billion to $3.6 billion, about 15 times the original budget. The Shoreham plant will

"The Shoreham plant will generate
at most one-third of the utility's electricity,
but its cost exceeds the book value
of Lilco's entire electricity system."

generate at most one-third of the utility's electricity, but its cost exceeds the book value of Lilco's entire electricity system. With the prospect of having to raise electricity rates by at least 60 percent, the utility commission is looking for ways to refinance the debt and phase in rate increases. Lilco may even try to sell the plant to the state, which would pay for it by issuing tax exempt bonds—thereby forcing federal taxpayers to bear some of the burden. If the Shoreham plant is permitted to operate, which many observers now doubt, it will yield the most expensive electricity ever produced by a large central generating station.[83]

39

The worst nuclear financial disaster so far is that of the Washington Public Power Supply System (WPPSS). Formed in the late fifties as a joint agency, WPPSS pooled the resources of over 100 public utilities in the Pacific Northwest. In the early seventies, facing escalating power demand, WPPSS launched one of the largest nuclear construction projects ever. Five 1,000-megawatt-plus nuclear plants were begun, all to be financed by tax-exempt municipal bonds issued by the Supply System.

Projected costs for the badly mismanaged projects ballooned from $4 billion in 1974 to $24 billion in 1981. Most of the money for the plants was borrowed, and by 1980 the Supply System was issuing $200 million in bonds every 90 days. The total outstanding debt passed $8 billion. While costs escalated, electricity demand growth slowed, quashing the notion that the five plants were essential. By 1981, the financial condition of the Supply System had deteriorated badly and its directors canceled plants 4 and 5, on which more than $2 billion had already been spent. The Washington State Supreme Court ruled in June 1983 that contracts requiring municipal utilities to honor the bonds for the canceled plants were not legally binding, causing the Supply System to default on the bonds—the largest such default in U.S. history.[84]

Even without the court ruling, default was inevitable. WPPSS had already been forced to mothball two additional plants that are 63 percent and 75 percent complete. (The one plant still under construction is 98 percent complete and scheduled to begin generating power in 1984.) It is a crisis of epic proportions. Among the casualties of the collapse are several thousand laid-off workers, the financial health of many energy-intensive farms and industries, and the municipal bond market itself, which has lost its risk-free image.

As striking as the depth of the WPPSS financial problems is the failure to respond earlier. Evidence mounted throughout the seventies that costs were soaring. As early as 1977 studies showed that cost-effective conservation measures could eliminate the need for two of the plants. But the utilities instead heeded the warnings of the federal Bonneville Power Administration that massive blackouts could occur without the five nuclear plants. Wall Street gave the bonds strong credit ratings and marketed them aggressively. The result was a circle of reinforcing misconceptions. Speaking of his fellow directors, WPPSS Chairman Carl Halvorson said, "They became captives of the mystique of the nuke. And they had unlimited money. That was the worst of it." A chagrined analyst at T. Rowe Price Associates Inc. said, "There has been an awful lot of blind faith in contract terms in the market generally and insufficient attention paid to the economic viability of the projects and the financial condition of issuers."[85]

Lack of attention to economic viability and abdication of responsibility by decision makers explains many of the problems plaguing nuclear power. Further clouding the nuclear "market" are major government subsidies. Recent studies put total U.S. Government spending for nuclear power development in the past three decades at between $15 billion and $46 billion (1982 dollars), depending on the accounting methods used. Almost two-thirds of the total is for reactor research and development (R&D). Other big-ticket items include subsidies for enriched uranium, nuclear waste disposal R&D, and subsidized sales abroad through low-interest loans of the Export-Import Bank. If utilities directly paid these costs, including breeder reactor development, it is estimated that nuclear electricity would be 50 percent more expensive.[86]

Not included in these figures are gaping tax loopholes for utilities that probably exceed all other subsidies combined. Investment tax credits and accelerated depreciation of assets allow utility companies to pay little taxes. Because the utility business is the most capital-intensive industry in the world, and because nuclear power is the most capital-intensive part of that business, such tax breaks are an enormous subsidy for nuclear investment. Although these incentives cannot be quantified precisely, Cornell University economist Duane Chapman concluded in 1980 that almost a third of the cost of nuclear plants is paid for by federal tax subsidies, compared to one-sixth for fossil-fuel-fired power plants.[87] The U.S. utility industry as a whole has an effective tax rate of only 9-11 percent after using available loopholes, according to a study by the Environmental Action Foundation.[88]

Another subsidy to nuclear power is tax breaks for capital invested in plants that are never completed. In addition to the $10 billion worth of plants canceled since the mid-seventies, the Department of Energy projects that between $4.5 billion and $8.1 billion of additional plants will be canceled in coming years. (The actual total will likely be higher still.) Regulatory battles are frequently fought over whether ratepayers or stockholders should pay these costs. Recent studies, however, show that about 40 percent is paid for by taxpayers in the form of tax deductions when utilities write off the lost investment on their tax returns—a $4 billion dollar write-off in the past decade.[89]

Also crucial to the U.S. nuclear industry is the Price-Anderson Act, passed by Congress in 1957. It established a $560 million limit on the liability of a nuclear plant's builder and operator for any damage the plant might cause. Experts agree that a serious nuclear accident could result in damage mounting to tens of billions of dollars—for which private insurance cannot be purchased. (Every insurance company has a nuclear exclusion clause in its contracts.) When the Price-Anderson Act became law the perceived risks of nuclear power were so great that the industry would not proceed without an exemption from the liability laws that govern all other industries. But members of Congress and the staff of the Nuclear Regulatory Commission have recently proposed abolishing the Price-Anderson Act. They view it as inappropriate for an industry now 20 years old and as a disincentive for reliable operation of nuclear plants. What terminating the Price-Anderson Act would do to the nuclear industry is unclear, but it would certainly bring nuclear power closer to the real economic world.[90]

Even with these enormous incentives, revival of nuclear orders in the United States does not appear imminent. In the past several years, utilities have scrambled to adjust their nuclear construction programs to changing conditions, but the economics has been so confused and lines of responsibility so uncertain that many decision makers have intervened too late. The financial crisis caused by the remaining nuclear projects hardly creates a climate conducive to contemplating major new investment programs.

The U.S. Atomic Industrial Forum began a 1982 press release with the assertion that, "The U.S. nuclear power program enters the home stretch of 1982 like a runner poised in mid-stride."[91] But the positive indicators the industry points to are the number of plants entering service and the power they generate—each of which continues to lag earlier projections by wide margins. No longer is the industry offering predictions of when it might stop living off pre-1975 plants and start ordering new ones. Perhaps the most bullish recent forecast is the Department of Energy's 1982 "mid-case" projection for the year 2000, which assumes that another 25 nuclear plants will be ordered in the eighties. This projection is probably little more than fantasy, however.[92] Serious analysts who expect to see additional nuclear orders before 1990 are hard to find.

The list of industry "preconditions" for the revival of nuclear power is usually dominated by regulatory reform, higher electricity rates to pay for the plants while they are being built, and lower inflation and interest rates. These issues, however, hardly scratch the surface of the industry's problems. The fundamental changes that are really needed—a guaranteed reduction in nuclear construction costs and a major surge in electricity growth—are far less likely.

With nuclear power much more expensive than available alternatives, even under the most favorable assumptions, and with the enormous financial risks a utility must now take to invest in nuclear power, additional orders in this decade are almost inconceivable. To encourage new orders, nuclear power development would have to be restructured—in other words, further removed from market discipline. Government would have to bear more of the burden. Bertram Wolfe, a vice-president in charge of the nuclear division of the General Electric Company, represents a growing mood in the nuclear industry when he says, "I just don't think you're going to see a revival of nuclear power until there's much stronger government involvement in the business."[93] The nuclear capitalists are now in full retreat.

"Serious analysts who expect
to see additional nuclear orders
before 1990 are hard to find."

The International Outlook

The financial collapse of nuclear power in the United States may be particularly severe, but it is not unique. Countries around the world have encountered problems that have slowed the pace of development, and many have trimmed their plans for the future. Although most governments with major nuclear programs remain strongly committed to nuclear power, the gap is widening between the money and talk spent on nuclear power and actual achievements. Behind the lagging pace lies a varied list of technical, economic and political problems and a diminished rate of growth of electricity demand.

Total nuclear power plans in Western Europe have risen only 10 percent since 1978, with most of the gains coming from France. The total nuclear commitments of Great Britain and West Germany have risen slightly, while those of Spain, Sweden, Switzerland and Italy have fallen. The changed outlook is well illustrated by the Organisation for Economic Co-operation and Development's nuclear capacity projections for 1985, which have been lowered by nearly two-thirds since 1970. (See Figure 6.)[94] Nuclear power's future in Europe, however, may be even more limited than these figures indicate.

In West Germany the private sector plays a major role in the direction of nuclear power programs, but authority is considerably more centralized than in the United States. The utility industry is dominated by a handful of large investor-owned companies that strongly support nuclear power and direct much of the planning in conjunction with the country's powerful private banks. Key government and business leaders have maintained their strong support of nuclear power throughout the last decade, and the nuclear program, including the development of a breeder reactor, continues to dominate the country's energy investments.[95]

Political opposition to nuclear power in West Germany has mushroomed since the late seventies. It is part of a broader questioning of the future of German society, spearheaded by the country's Green Party, which has made the dissolution of the nuclear power program its top priority after the elimination of nuclear missiles in Europe. Major demonstrations have occurred at many nuclear plant sites, including one near Hamburg in 1981 that the West German Interior

Minister described as the biggest police action in the history of the Federal Republic.[96]

Much of the opposition to nuclear power arises out of local concern about proposed nuclear plants. In West Germany, the länder (state) governments have the final say on nuclear licensing decisions, and opponents have successfully raised issues of safety, environmental damage and cost-effectiveness at hearings and in the courts. Design standards have been frequently upgraded and many plants altered substantially. As a result, project delays and cost overruns closely

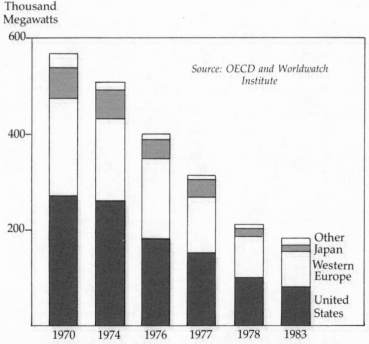

Figure 6: Projections of 1985 Nuclear Generating Capacity in the Western Nations and Japan by Year of Projection

parallel those in the United States. Meanwhile, electricity growth rates have dropped substantially, and the country's economy has faltered, making investment in major capital-intensive projects much less attractive.[97]

Only one nuclear power plant has been ordered in West Germany since 1975, and construction has not yet begun on eight ordered before 1975, largely because of political opposition and ongoing court battles. Only eight nuclear plants are under construction, four of them at least 80 percent complete and another three at least 50 percent complete. The West German nuclear industry suffers from considerable overcapacity, and component manufacturers are reportedly losing a good deal of money. Kraftwerk Union, a subsidiary of the Siemens electronics conglomerate, manufactures West Germany's reactors and is reportedly suffering losses on nuclear power. Many workers have been laid off, and without new orders, the West German nuclear industry is expected to weaken rapidly.[98]

With only about 8,000 megawatts-worth of nuclear plants now under construction, West Germany in 1990 will have less than half the 45,000 megawatts of nuclear capacity projected in the mid-seventies. The West German nuclear program is at a crossroads, with the country's energy future beyond 1990 hanging in the balance. A "convoy" of largely standardized plants has received preliminary approval. Uncertain is whether this proposal can withstand criticism that the plants will be substantially more expensive than alternatives. Some utility officials now admit that the growing costs of nuclear power and a 50 percent reserve margin in most of the country's utility system offer little incentive to take major new risks.[99]

France is the only country with a major nuclear program keeping close to its ambitious plans of a decade ago. Prompted by the 1973 oil embargo, France ordered an average of six nuclear plants each year between 1974 and the early eighties and now has 30 nuclear plants in operation and 28 more under construction. France obtained 40 percent of its electricity from nuclear power in 1983 and is on course to reach 75 percent by 1990. By then the country will have 80 percent more nuclear generating capacity than it had total capacity in 1973. But, even with France's impressive six-year construction schedules and reputation for cost control, clouds now appear on the horizon.[100]

The nuclear business in France is run by two powerful government agencies, the French Atomic Energy Agency, responsible for research and development, fuel supply and waste disposal, and Electricité de France (EDF), the national utility that builds and operates the country's nuclear plants. Both report to the Ministry of Industry and their actions are fully coordinated. Even Framatome, the once-private company that builds all French nuclear reactors, is now half government-owned.[101]

The French nuclear program is a priority for the country's strong central government and industrial leaders. The income and jobs that nuclear power provides are a strong incentive to continue the program. Both the steel and heavy electrical industries, two important sectors of the economy, are heavily dependent on the nuclear program. Decision making is centralized and French courts give the sporadic political opposition to the nuclear program little opportunity to intervene. Government public relations campaigns dissuade local communities from opposing proposed plants. The staying power of the French nuclear program was demonstrated in 1981 when Socialist President Mitterand called the nuclear program "excessive, even dangerous" during his campaign and then supported nuclear power strongly after his election.[102]

Economic realities have proved much more hazardous to the French nuclear program than political opposition. Electricity growth has been gradually slowing since the late seventies, and the government, projecting annual growth in electricity demand of 5.6 percent as recently as 1981, finally reduced its 1990 growth forecast by 50 percent in 1982. These new figures mean that France will have at least 13 percent too much generating capacity in 1990. Furthermore, the country may be generating well over 80 percent of its electricity from nuclear power. Such a high proportion means that some nuclear plants must be used intermittently to match fluctuating daily demand (a role usually reserved for hydro and fossil fuel plants). This poses a major technical challenge and hurts the economics of nuclear power.[103]

To ensure a market for all of the additional generating capacity, EDF now offers special subsidies for electric heating and has set up regional agencies to encourage industries to use more power. Also

"In 1982 the director
of Electricité de France said that
the utility was in worse financial condition
than it had been for 30 years."

planned are shutdowns of many relatively new coal-fired plants and the export of electricity.[104] An additional crunch is coming as nuclear programs burden already strained capital markets. The French Atomic Energy Agency now has an annual budget of over FF 10 billion, or between $1.5 billion and $2 billion. EDF lost approximately FF 8 billion in 1982 and has accumulated a total debt of FF 152 billion, although part of the debt was forgiven by the government in 1981. Debt reschedulings and major borrowing on the Eurobond market have been required to keep construction going. In 1982 the director of EDF said that the utility was in worse financial condition than it had been for 30 years. Since EDF is government-owned, French taxpayers will likely pay a large share of the debt.[105]

47

In 1983 a high-level government committee published a study concluding that the country would need no additional nuclear plant orders until 1987. Recognizing the damage this would do to an industry geared to handle six new orders per year, the government has reduced nuclear plant orders to two units per year in 1984 and 1985. Even this plan threatens massive layoffs of nuclear workers and could force France's small nuclear supplier companies out of business. A reduced pace of ordering would also disrupt the economy and the famed efficiency of the French program. Already Framatome has quoted costs 20 to 40 percent higher should ordering be cut to two per year.[106]

The French nuclear program, though successful politically and in narrow economic terms, has also been hurt by its own success. Its large scale and the dearth of political opposition have helped reduce costs but have also made it hard to adjust to economic difficulties and lower electricity demand. The future of nuclear power in France will be decided largely on political grounds, but France's leaders will find it increasingly hard to justify ordering even two units per year. European nuclear analysts William Walker and Måns Lönnroth, analyzing the French nuclear industry, concluded in 1983 that, "It risks a vicious circle of rising costs, higher electricity prices and even lower growth rates. A long period of drought therefore seems imminent for the French nuclear industry."[107] In the nineties France will almost certainly be generating more nuclear electricity per person than any other country, but by then this last full-throttle nuclear expansion effort may have sputtered to a halt.

The British nuclear program is much more anemic. Beyond the 8,500 megawatts of nuclear power now supplying 13 percent of the country's electricity, only another 5,500 megawatts-worth are under construction, most of it nearing completion. The high cost of British nuclear plants built so far and forecasts that electricity demand will be steady or even fall in the next decade provide ample economic hurdles to a revitalized nuclear construction program. The ongoing Sizewell Inquiry on whether to build an American-style light water plant provides the only hope for additional nuclear orders in the near future. Unless the plan proceeds, the nuclear industry in Britain will soon wither. And even if Britain should decide to build a light water plant, its ability to support a vital nuclear industry seems doubtful.[108]

Nuclear power programs in other northern European countries are quite small and unlikely to grow significantly in the near future. Belgium has five operating nuclear plants, Finland four, Switzerland four and the Netherlands two, but only Belgium has additional plants being built. None of these countries has a pressing need for more generating capacity, and many national leaders now question the rationale for additional nuclear plants.[109] New orders do not appear imminent. Sweden aggressively developed nuclear power until 1980, when a national referendum discontinued its construction program and called for closing all the country's nuclear power plants by the year 2010. Although Sweden has nine reactors in operation and gets over 30 percent of its electricity from nuclear power, only two plants are still being built.[110]

The nuclear power programs of the Soviet Union and Eastern Europe, largely independent of those in the West, have followed a surprisingly parallel course. Nuclear plant construction in the Soviet Union began in earnest in the early seventies, and the nation's nuclear capacity grew from 1,600 megawatts in 1970 to 6,200 megawatts in 1975 and 17,500 megawatts (at 29 plants) in 1983. Nuclear power is run and controlled by the Soviet Government and the Communist Party, which consider electrification to be the foundation of a modern economy. State-owned companies design and build the plants, state utilities operate them, and government officials determine in their Five-Year Plans how many reactors will be financed.[111]

"The Soviet Union currently obtains
about half as much electricity
from its nuclear plants
as was projected a decade ago."

Since the late seventies, the Soviet nuclear program has focused on its Atommash plant, designed to produce as many as eight standardized nuclear reactors each year. This unprecedented effort at nuclear standardization is supposed to help cut project lead times and reduce costs. The Atommash Plant is part of the only internationally integrated nuclear program, in which components made in various Eastern European facilities are used in each plant. The large Skoda facility in Czechoslovakia produces turbines, generators, pumps and pipelines. Plants in Hungary, Bulgaria, East Germany and Poland are also involved.[112]

49

As with much of the Soviet economy, the nuclear program is kept under tight wraps. Published information accentuates successes and downplays problems. (Problems encountered by Western nuclear programs, including the Three Mile Island accident, are well-publicized and regarded as examples of the failures of capitalism.) Reports have emerged nonetheless of technical and organizational difficulties slowing the pace of nuclear development, including labor-management problems and delays caused by builders and suppliers. The nuclear targets in the current Five-Year Plan will reportedly be missed by at least 6,000 megawatts. In 1982 the Central Committee reorganized the nuclear program, hoping to improve its efficiency. The Atommash facility itself is at least two or three years behind schedule, and it suffered a major accident in mid-1983. Full capacity is not expected until 1990 at the earliest.[113]

Such problems are by no means rare in the Soviet economy, but the scale of the nuclear setbacks is unusual. The Soviet Union currently obtains about half as much electricity from its nuclear plants as was projected a decade ago, and the rest of Eastern Europe has missed its targets by similar margins. Nuclear power is nonetheless becoming an increasingly important energy source throughout the Eastern bloc, already supplying 6 percent of the Soviet Union's electricity, 12 percent of East Germany's and 18 percent of Bulgaria's.

Official projections call for nuclear power to supply close to a third of the region's electricity by 1990, which would require at least a tripling of nuclear capacity.[114] Recent delays and cost overruns are likely to cause these goals to be missed as well. A time of testing almost certainly lies ahead for Eastern Europe's nuclear power programs since the scale of the efforts and the consequent financial and technical risks are growing rapidly. Massive centralization and the absence of political opposition and financial checks are likely to cause more problems than solutions, but it will be some years before the performance of Eastern Europe's nuclear program can be fully assessed by outsiders.

Japan has one of the largest nuclear development programs in the world today. Despite the painful legacy of the atomic bomb and considerable fear of radiation, nuclear power has been a cornerstone of government energy policy since the early seventies. With 117 million people squeezed into an area the size of California and four-fifths of the country's energy currently imported, nuclear power is viewed as the only means of rapidly enhancing national energy security. Japan has 25 nuclear plants in operation that supply 16 percent of the country's electricity, and another 13 are under way. Japan has ambitious plans to expand nuclear capacity sixfold by the end of the century, at which point nuclear power would provide about half of the country's electricity.[115]

The first nuclear plants in Japan, based on U.S. designs, were built in conjunction with overseas corporations. Major R&D efforts in recent years have aimed for an independent nuclear technology and industry, a process now largely complete. Today Japan is considered a leader in reactor technology and has initiated joint ventures with U.S. and West German companies to develop an advanced light water reactor design.[116] Japanese companies apparently aim to compete in the nuclear export market should it revive in the years ahead.

The Japanese nuclear program is threatened mainly by political opposition, which grows as the number of communities affected by nuclear plants increases. Becauase Japan is so small and crowded, nuclear plants inevitably infringe on someone's "backyard," often a valuable fishery or beach resort. Radiation accidentally released at one nuclear plant has aroused enormous concern. Also troublesome are frequent earthquakes—which could severely damage nuclear plants in virtually all parts of Japan—and nuclear waste disposal, a particularly hard problem to resolve in such a populous country.[117]

Japan has failed to meet its early nuclear goals by a large margin. The target for 1995, for example, has already been reduced by 13,000 megawatts, and the recent recession may further delay the nuclear program. Cost overruns apparently concern Japan's nuclear managers, but not enough to force a wholesale reevaluation of the country's nuclear goals. Also troubling are frequent shutdowns and what until recently was one of the worst nuclear operating records worldwide. These problems were seemingly resolved in 1982, but whether this improved record will last is uncertain. Although the country's energy officials are determined to forge ahead, their pace will probably be limited by plant operating and safety records and by success in dealing with the waste disposal problem.[118]

Developing countries had some of the brightest hopes for nuclear power in the sixties and seventies. Third World leaders viewed nuclear power as the prototypical modern technology and as a way to boost national prestige and reduce crippling oil import bills. Governments and international agencies in industrial countries dispatched experts to promote the economic merits of nuclear power. In the early seventies, the International Atomic Energy Agency (IAEA) projected that developing countries would have 550,000 megawatts of nuclear capacity by the end of the century—40 percent more than worldwide operating and planned nuclear capacity in 1983.[119]

By mid-1983 six developing countries—Taiwan, South Korea, India, Pakistan, South Africa and Argentina—had a total of 13 operating nuclear plants. Three more developing countries are building plants and several others are considering nuclear programs. But the Third World has just 6 percent of the total worldwide commitment to nuclear power. And since the mid-seventies the nuclear plans of developing countries have been substantially reduced. Many nations regard nuclear power as important only in the distant future, and others have eliminated it from long-range planning altogether. As in the industrial countries, nuclear power's problems in the developing world are largely economic.[120]

A key obstacle to nuclear development is the small size of electricity grids in Third World countries. If a single power plant provides more than 15 percent of a grid's capacity, the whole system will "crash" if that plant is shut down. Using these figures, the IAEA estimates that only South Korea, Taiwan, Pakistan and India have grids large enough to install a conventional 1000-megawatt nuclear power plant, and only a few more countries will reach that point in the next decade.[121]

Nuclear manufacturers have responded by proposing "mini-reactors" in the range of 100-500 megawatts. Research on small reactors has been done in Canada, France, Japan, Sweden, the United States and West Germany, but early plans have been continually pushed back. Only the Soviet Union currently has mini-reactors, but it does not export them. The estimated per-kilowatt construction cost for a nuclear plant of 200 megawatts is more than twice that of a 1000-megawatt plant. This means that a U.S. company marketing such a plant in a developing country would have to charge at least $4,000 per kilowatt of installed capacity (1982 dollars), which exceeds the cost of available alternatives.[122]

A deteriorating world economy since 1980 has also led to a significant trimming of the Third World's most active nuclear power programs. The capital intensity of nuclear power plants makes them unattractive to debt-strapped developing countries, particularly since much of the capital must be spent abroad, draining scarce foreign exchange. Substituting nuclear import bills for oil import bills is not seen as much of a gain by most Third World leaders.

The "miracle economies" of the Far East have made the largest commitments to nuclear power in the Third World. Rapid growth and sizable electricity grids in countries such as South Korea and Taiwan explain why they are likely to have over half of the Third World's nuclear capacity in 1990. Taiwan, clinging to an aggressive nuclear expansion program begun in the seventies, has four operating plants and two under construction. The pace slackened in 1982, however, when Taiwan deferred several reactors indefinitely because of economic constraints and a slowdown in electricity growth.[123] South Korea has two operating plants and seven under construction, but it has also decided against new orders in the early eighties.[124] National leaders in these countries are strongly commited to nuclear power, but a major improvement in economic conditions is now a prerequisite to building additional plants.

"The capital intensity
of nuclear power plants makes them
unattractive to debt-strapped
developing countries."

The Philippines once had ambitious plans for nuclear power, but the country's first plant, sited near an earthquake fault, suffered major delays and cost overruns while the seismic design was bolstered. Plans for additional plants have been scrapped.[125] Thailand and Indonesia are reportedly considering nuclear power plants, but their entry into the nuclear world is still problematic. China has yet to begin building a nuclear plant, but the potential size of this market is eyed lustfully by nuclear manufacturers. Some of China's leaders appear quite interested in nuclear power, but capital requirements have made them cautious in beginning major commitments. So far China has ordered only one small nuclear plant, and if the country's program goes forward, it will likely be at a slow pace.[126]

India has the broadest range of nuclear technology and expertise of any Third World country. Its nuclear power program is largely homegrown and much more independent than those of other developing nations. Four small plants are operating and another six are under construction. India now expects to obtain 10 percent of electricity from nuclear power by the nineties. But the early hopes of the country's nuclear scientists have not been realized. The plants are expensive and have poor operating records. Additional orders are not foreseen in the near future.[127]

Among the Middle Eastern countries that once had ambitious plans for nuclear power are Egypt, Iran, Iraq and Pakistan. Each has seen a combination of economic and political problems seriously jeopardize its nuclear programs. Iran's Islamic revolution in 1979 toppled an ambitious and costly nuclear power effort aimed at installing 23,000 megawatts of nuclear capacity by 1994. Even before the revolution, however, critics questioned the large scale and economic viability of the Iranian program. Iraq's nuclear program came to a halt in 1981 when Israeli warplanes destroyed the research reactor that was its centerpiece. Egypt and Pakistan also considered building nuclear plants in the eighties, but both those efforts are now on hold.[128]

Latin America was a booming market for nuclear power in the seventies, but it too has fallen on hard times. Argentina has had a small nuclear plant operating since the early seventies, and two more are being built. Wrapped in the cloak of nationalism, Argentina's nuclear program has enjoyed strong government support, and the country hopes to have six operating plants by the end of the century. Crippling debt problems, however, have cast doubt on Argentina's nuclear goals, and anything beyond the two plants now being built is uncertain.[129]

Brazil, the world's sixth most populous country, has one nuclear plant nearing operation and two under construction. The country planned to have eight plants operating by the early nineties, largely relying on West German technology, but major technical problems and a lack of capital have rendered these goals meaningless. Brazil will be lucky to complete the plants now under construction.[130] Mexico was a latecomer to nuclear power, but as oil revenues soared in 1979 and 1980, the country's leaders announced plans to build seven plants in the eighties. Today that vision has been obliterated by the country's debt crisis. The request for project bids was withdrawn in 1982, and Mexico now has just two plants under construction.[131]

Current plans indicate that developing countries will have at most 20,000 megawatts of nuclear capacity by 1990, or one-seventh as much as projected by the IAEA in the early seventies.[132] Yet even these numbers overrate the economic viability of nuclear power in developing countries. All of the nuclear sales in the Third World so far were subsidized by industrial country governments or manufacturers. The day when nuclear plants are sufficiently cost-effective that developing countries will buy them at the full price is far off indeed. And no commercially available nuclear technology can yet meet more than a few percent of the developing world's electricity needs.[133]

Beyond these problems lies the more fundamental question of whether nuclear power is a wise use of scarce resources for a developing country. Nuclear power creates fewer jobs and requires more dependence on foreign companies and governments than does almost any other investment a Third World nation can make.[134] Even assuming that nuclear power could be made cost-effective, the development of other energy sources would likely provide broader economic benefits. Nuclear power is also likely to serve a small minority that uses electricity while bypassing the majority who rely on fuelwood and charcoal. Investment in rural electrification using small-scale renewable energy sources, or improving the efficiency of wood cookstoves, would provide far greater benefits.

Nuclear power's aura of modernity has been replaced by an image of backwardness and mismanagement. Nuclear power was greatly over-sold in the Third World. Humanitarian and profit-seeking motives became confused, and projects were pushed that had little hope of being successful. The hardsell is continuing as industrial country officials attempt to bolster their flagging nuclear industries by selling more plants to developing countries.[135] Nuclear power in the Third World was stillborn, and most nations would benefit if those projects not yet started were swiftly canceled. Beyond the economic issue is the growing realization that even successfully completed nuclear power plants are inviting military and terrorist targets in politically unstable regions.

Worldwide, nuclear power development hangs by a much thinner thread than most policymakers yet realize. The global commitment to building nuclear power plants has declined by 31,000 megawatts since 1978, as major cancellations in the United States were not offset by modest orders in some other nations. Further declines in the next few years are virtually certain since few orders are expected, and most of the 20 to 30 plants not yet under construction or mothballed are candidates for cancellation. The eighties are shaping up as a disastrous decade for nuclear power, and the world's nuclear industries are already feeling the pain. The usually optimistic Nuclear Energy Agency of the OECD concluded in 1982 that, "There is some risk that the nuclear industry will not remain commercially viable in a climate of uncertain and variable markets." Markets of any kind are becoming rare indeed for the nuclear industry.[136]

Toward A Market Test

Evidence is compelling that nuclear power has lost economic ground during the past decade. In several nations, electricity from new nuclear power plants is significantly more expensive than electricity from new coal-fired plants. Where nuclear cost overruns have been relatively modest, nuclear power's economic advantages over coal are significant but not overwhelming. Even these comparisons overstate the likelihood that the industry will revive in the future. Fundamental changes in the economics of electricity are challenging past assumptions and expanding the list of options available to utilities. This broader context is what will likely determine nuclear power's future.

56 Some would argue that even if nuclear power is expensive it is still an essential energy source for replacing imported oil. While it is true that nuclear power has helped lower oil imports in some nations—particularly France and Japan—in most countries its contribution has been negligible, dwarfed by coal and energy efficiency. In the United States oil imports have fallen 50 percent since 1978, but nuclear power generation has risen only 5 percent. Today a small and shrinking fraction of the world's oil is used to generate electricity, and the oil versus nuclear equation is largely moot.[137]

The choice between coal or nuclear power as usually posed has many drawbacks. Coal-caused air pollution has steadily increased in many countries, producing new evidence of health and environmental damage. Air pollution is shortening the lives of millions of people, particularly in developing countries that cannot afford pollution controls. Energy costs have increased in industrial countries that strictly limit emissions from coal-fired power plants, though studies show that the health and environmental benefits of the controls are worth the price. Recently, acid rain and the threat of carbon-dioxide-caused climate change were added to the list of coal-related ills and appear much less open to simple technical fixes.[138]

The world's energy options, however, are not limited to a choice between nuclear power or coal. The biggest change in the utility industry in recent years has been the new role of "end use" energy efficiency as an alternative to new power plants of any kind. By increasing the amount of light delivered by a light bulb or the work performed by an industrial motor for every kilowatt-hour of electricity used, the same energy services are gained at a lower cost than is possible with a new generating plant. Throughout the world, dozens of energy efficiency studies have been sponsored by research institutes, universities and private companies. These studies, whether examining the economy as a whole or particular sectors such as housing or steel production, conclude that improved energy efficiency has enormous untapped potential.

"In the United States
oil imports have fallen 50 percent since 1978,
but nuclear power generation
has risen only 5 percent."

A 1981 report by the U.S. Solar Energy Research Institute estimated that cost-effective investment in energy efficiency could reduce the rate of growth of electricity use from 3.5 percent per year to less than 0.5 percent per year for the rest of the century while the economy surged ahead at a 4 percent annual growth rate. The Northwest Conservation and Electric Power Plan, ordered by the U.S. Congress in response to the region's nuclear power problems, concluded that conservation could hold electricity use to current levels for the rest of the century. A 1983 analysis by Earth Resources Research in Great Britain found that a somewhat more ambitious assortment of energy efficiency measures could reduce British electricity use by 48 percent by 2025 while the country's gross national product doubled.[139]

A 1983 study by Howard Geller of the American Council for an Energy-Efficient Economy graphically illustrates the potential for specific energy efficiency improvements to trim power use. The report concludes that by replacing residential appliances in use today with more efficient models already on the market, power demand could be reduced by 64,000 megawatts—about equal to 1983 U.S. nuclear capacity. The need for 13 1,000-megawatt nuclear plants could be eliminated just by shifting to more efficient refrigerators, and 12 more could be dropped by replacing all light bulbs with more efficient ones.[140]

In the current era of steeply rising costs, "end use" energy efficiency is the only major bargain available to the utility industry. Many of today's efficiency investments save energy at a cost of between 1¢ and 2¢ per kilowatt-hour, or a tenth to a fifth the cost of electricity from a new coal or nuclear plant.[141] Since the mid-seventies skyrocketing electric rates have caused a blossoming in efficiency innovations and marketing. Some older technologies are just now benefiting from the scientific achievements of the late twentieth century. One example is computer-controlled industrial equipment and building energy systems that always supply power at the most efficient rate.

U.S. investments in energy efficiency in 1982 hit $9 billion, yet they are only one-seventh of the cost-effective level, according to estimates by the Mellon Energy Productivity Institute.[142] Nevertheless, the utility industry has been slow to redefine its role. Fortunes have been made and careers established largely on the basis of successful completion of ever-larger power plants. In addition, tax codes and regulatory incentives penalize utilities that depart from the "build at any cost—so long as it is in the rate base" philosophy.

Attitudes are beginning to change, however. A 1983 survey of 120 U.S. utilities by the Investor Responsibility Research Center (IRRC) found that 75 percent have formal energy efficiency programs and two-thirds practice "load management" (shifting power demand away from peak periods to reduce the need for new generating capacity). Some provide loans or even grants for insulation or storm windows. Others lend money to buy more efficient appliances. Collectively the 120 utilities surveyed estimate that improved efficiency will reduce their need for new generating capacity by 30,000 megawatts over the next decade, at a cost of $6.6 billion, or less than one-sixth the cost of equivalent power from a new nuclear plant.[143]

Dozens of studies and years of lobbying by citizens groups have prompted regulators to require efficiency programs and to include these investments in the rate base. In the late seventies, the Environmental Defense Fund argued for a redirection of California utility strategies toward conservation and small-scale generating technologies. This approach was later adopted by the California Public Utilities Commission and utility executives who saw improved efficiency as being in their own financial interest. Over-extended capital spending, mainly for nuclear projects, has led many utilities to make reduced investment a priority. Donald Jordan, president of the Edison Electric Institute, said in 1983, "The huge construction program we face has damaged our industry. . . The best thing for us would be no growth." Five years ago the utility industry might have charged Jordan with blasphemy.[144]

Energy conservation programs have caught on more slowly outside the United States, but many are now beginning. Virtually throughout the industrial world electricity growth rates have slipped from the 6-8 percent annual rate of the early seventies to between 1 and 4 percent today. In most industrial countries electricity use apparently will grow at a slower pace than does gross national product. In much of Northern Europe, electricity use could actually decline.[145]

Utilities still resisting the idea of electricity as a market commodity whose role varies according to price are often those with the largest commitments to nuclear power. Utility planners in France, for example, encourage electricity demand so that it will match the growing supply and justify earlier decisions to order the plants. However, most utilities, including Electricité de France, have had to raise rates to pay for new plants, and this encourages consumers to conserve. As a result, many nuclear plants sow the seeds of their own economic demise. With only modest efficiency programs, most utilities in industrial countries could avoid building any new power plants for at least a decade.

When new generating capacity is needed, utilities will have many more options than when they last ordered plants. Promising renewable energy sources include small-scale hydropower, geothermal energy, biomass energy, wind power and photovoltaic solar energy. In addition, cogeneration—the combined production of heat and power—is a rapidly growing alternative to central power plants. The cost of these energy sources today ranges from just below to substantially higher than the cost of power from new coal or nuclear plants. But the cost of these new power sources is declining steadily while coal and nuclear costs are still rising. (See Table 3.)[146]

Table 3: Estimated Cost of Electricity from New Plants, 1983, with Projections for 1990*

Energy Source	1983	1990
	(cents per kilowatt-hour)	
Nuclear Power	10-12	14-16
Coal	5-7	7-9
Small Hydropower	8-10	10-12
Cogeneration	4-6	4-6
Biomass	8-15	7-10
Wind Power	12-20	6-10
Photovoltaics	50-100	10-20
Energy Efficiency	1-2	3-5

*Costs expressed in 1982 dollars.
Source: Worldwatch Institute.

Since 1980 some of the new energy sources have moved from the laboratory to the marketplace, mostly on a limited scale. The Philippines leads in biomass-fueled power plants, West Germany in cogeneration, China, El Salvador and Nepal in small hydropower, and the United States and Denmark in wind generation. Photovoltaic cells, now the most expensive renewable energy technology, have been falling in price the fastest, and the solar cell market has grown thirtyfold since 1977. Over 50 U.S. utilities have invested in new generating sources or are buying power from independent small power producers. The utilities have plans to add 15,000 megawatts of generating capacity from these sources by the year 2000, a conservative estimate since many utilities are still formulating plans.[147]

Most new generating sources can be developed on a small scale with short lead times, avoiding the enormous financial risks posed by a 1,000-megawatt power plant. A wind farm or a solar plant can be built on almost any scale and plans quickly modified if demand shifts, an important advantage since utility forecasters have shown almost no facility for accurate projections. Photovoltaic technology has been developed in the laboratory and become a commercial reality in less time than it takes to plan and build a single nuclear plant. A spokesperson for the Southern California Edison Company, a pioneer in nuclear power in the sixties and now a leader in harnessing renewable energy sources, said, "The age of the dinosaur—the large central power plant with a 10-to-15 year lead time—may have passed."[148]

Alternative power sources will supply only between 3 and 5 percent of projected U.S. generating capacity at the end of the century, but they will meet a large part of the modest additions to power demand, and their value goes beyond the number of megawatts supplied. Renewable energy developers bring a spirit of innovation to the utility industry, where gradually, as in any other business, price is becoming important and losers bear the burden of their mistakes.

Nuclear power will find it hard to survive in the competitive economic climate taking hold. In the United States most utilities now state openly that they do not even consider nuclear power in planning new generating capacity for the next decade. In other countries the strength of nuclear development appears to decline in direct proportion to the degree of responsibility and risk the private sector is required to assume. Centrally planned economies such as those of France and the Soviet Union, which protect nuclear power both from economic pressures and outside critics, have continued to expand the role of nuclear power. In West Germany, where nuclear power is more closely tied to the private sector, plans have dwindled. Where nuclear power must face a market test, it has generally failed.

If an overriding national goal is the expansion of nuclear power, a centrally planned energy program appears to be best. However, providing energy services at the least cost and ensuring adequate capital for non-energy investments make a centralized commitment to nuclear power much less attractive. Even the relatively successful nuclear power programs are encountering cost overruns that cannot be entirely short-circuited via central planning.

Innovative efficiency programs and renewable energy projects have been slow to develop in countries where utility planning is centralized and small entrepreneurs play no role. Such countries may fall far behind in areas where technological improvements are progressing most rapidly. But to keep nuclear power expanding, planners must devote virtually all resources to nuclear development. Efficiency investments are feared because they compete with the near total commitment nuclear power needs. Once nuclear power is protected from market forces, the process can easily become complex and insidious. Not only are other alternatives squelched but the pressure to misrepresent economic issues and hide technical problems becomes enormous.

Experience so far indicates that a government commitment to nuclear power must be absolute and unending to be successful, preconditions that raise many issues beyond energy policy ones. If nuclear power cannot be developed without complete protection from the market, many countries would have to restructure their economies and even alter the rights of citizens to have a successful nuclear power program.

The economic failings of nuclear power suggest the need for several major policy changes. First is a more balanced approach in energy research and development (R&D), which nuclear power has dominated in most industrial countries since the fifties. Fossil fuel combustion, energy efficiency and renewable energy technologies each deserve a share of energy R&D roughly equal to that given nuclear power. Already, private energy R&D spending has shifted dramatically in this direction, and some governments are following suit.[149]

Resources are also misdirected within nuclear R&D programs. Most funds have gone to breeder reactor technologies, viewed for the past two decades as the inevitable next evolutionary stage for nuclear power. Breeder reactors produce new nuclear fuel while they generate power, removing the worry that uranium fuel will run out. But uranium prices and supplies have played no part in the current problems of nuclear power, and the breeder reactor development programs have not been aimed at resolving fundamental issues of safety and cost. In fact, breeder reactors promise to be significantly more complex and possibly more vulnerable to catastrophic accidents than light water reactors.[150] The cancellation of the $3 billion Clinch River breeder reactor project in the United States in 1983 was a step in the right direction. Nuclear R&D could be productively redirected to finding safe ways to dispose of nuclear wastes and to decommission old reactors.

Countries that want to develop nuclear power in the future will need simpler fail-safe reactor technologies that do not yet exist. One of the chief lessons of the nuclear power experience so far is that existing technologies cannot provide sufficient safety at a reasonable cost. Many of the strongest advocates of nuclear power now argue that engineers and physists will need to design new plants. Some small steps in this direction have begun, principally in Japan. This is the only way nuclear power could possibly become economical. But success of such programs is not guaranteed, and they could become multi-billion-dollar dry holes.

Improving the analytical base on which utility industry investments are made is as important as redirecting R&D programs. Failing to anticipate the slower rate of growth in electricity use in the seventies was a mistake of monumental proportions. Although some mistakes are inevitable, planners took far longer to adjust to the change than they should have. Similarly, power plant cost projections have been uniformly low, a consistency that should itself provide a warning flag.

"Without a range of incentives
to encourage better performance,
the economics of nuclear
power cannot improve."

To be effective, forecasters and analysts must resist political pressures and examine the real world, not simply extrapolate historical trends.

Regulatory reforms are in order, both for nuclear manufacturers and the utility industry. As part of a move to standardize reactor design and improve safety, the review process can be streamlined and paperwork reduced. This should save some time and money, though not nearly as much as the nuclear industry has hoped. Enough generic technical problems and uncertainties remain in nuclear power plants that any decision to "freeze" the regulatory process and prevent the introduction of new standards would create more problems than it would solve.

Rate commissions, through their control over spending, must provide more incentives for utilities to build plants cheaply and operate them safely and efficiently. Higher rates should be granted for plants built on time and within budget. In a pioneering move, the California Public Utilities Commission voted in 1983 to fine utilities whose plants operate below a 55 percent capacity factor and reward those that go above 80 percent.[15] The utility industry usually approaches "regulatory reform" by arguing for higher rates, but automatically authorizing revenue for projects with huge cost overruns and questionable performance makes little economic sense and is not in the best interest of ratepayers.

What the nuclear industy needs most is a good dose of market discipline. Without a range of incentives to encourage better performance, the economics of nuclear power cannot improve. One step would be to change tax codes that provide too high a reward for capital investment in new power plants. Another would be to reform nuclear liability laws to ensure an adequate financial incentive for the safe operation of nuclear power plants.

Also needed are changes in the contracts between utilities and the builders of nuclear plants. Controlling costs will be impossible until the day of the open-ended, cost-plus contract is brought to a close and contractors are prohibited from making a profit on cost overruns. Eventually, regulators may wish to consider granting power plant builders standard marginal electricity rates for any additional power generated. Builders would take responsibility for deciding which power sources to develop, but would also shoulder the financial risk should the project cost more than expected. Interestingly, these are the same provisions granted to small power producers developing many renewable energy sources in the United States.

Nuclear power's protected status, apart from all other energy sources, is no longer justified. The broad variety of alternatives available and the pace at which the utility industry is changing make a balanced approach more important than ever. Attempts to pick out a single energy source and direct the pace of development are bound to fail. Adequate power at the lowest feasible price is the most sensible overall goal, with an internal accounting of the environmental effects and risks associated with each energy source. Nuclear power may not pass this market test, but if not, it will be replaced by more appropriate energy sources.

Nuclear power's economic problems are not about to disappear. Costs continue to increase in all countries, and high interest rates and tight capital markets will likely remain, even with a vigorous economic recovery. Arguments over the economics of nuclear power will likely grow more heated as nuclear cost increases begin to affect electricity consumers directly, and as nuclear industries, starved for new orders, pressure for more support.

The question now is not whether to make a few small adjustments to further encourage a thriving industry, but whether to introduce fundamental institutional changes and new economic subsidies to prop up a dying business. Leaders in many countries will be tempted to muddle through, making one decision at a time and so wading gradually into a financial quagmire. This could be the most costly approach of all. Slowly dying nuclear programs are likely to have a hard time attracting first-rate management and engineering talent. Further cost overruns and more accidents could result. Whether nuclear programs expand or not, many societies will have to devote considerable effort to solving problems posed by slowly aging nuclear plants and their attendant waste products.

National leaders continue to be mesmerized by the once-great hopes placed in nuclear power and fail to assess its economic performance objectively. A basic business principle holds that money-losing enterprises should not be continued in an attempt to recover early losses if more promising investment opportunities are available. The time is at hand to decide whether nuclear power programs have reached this point. Many nations would benefit by cutting their losses and moving on to more productive endeavors.

Notes

1. International Energy Agency, *World Energy Outlook* (Paris: Organisation for Economic Co-operation and Development, 1982); U.S. Atomic Energy Commission, *Nuclear Power Growth 1973-2000* (Washington, D.C.: 1971).

2. International Atomic Energy Agency, *The Annual Report for 1982* (Vienna: 1983).

3. American Nuclear Society, "The World List of Nuclear Power Plants," *Nuclear News*, August 1983; "Nuclear: World Status," *Financial Times Energy Economist*, January 1983; Atomic Industrial Forum, "International Survey— Annual," Washington, D.C., March 1983.

4. "Nuclear: World Status," *Financial Times Energy Economist*, January 1983.

5. Ralph E. Lapp, *The New Force* (New York: Harper & Brothers, 1953); David Dietz, *Atomic Energy in the Coming Era* (New York: Dodd Mead, 1945); Bertrand Goldschmidt, *The Atomic Complex: A Worldwide Political History of Nuclear Energy* (La Grange Park, Illinois: American Nuclear Society, 1982).

6. Peter deLeon, *Development and Diffusion of the Nuclear Power Reactor: A Comparative Analysis* (Cambridge, Mass.: Ballinger Publishing Co., 1979); Arnold Kramish, *Atomic Energy in the Soviet Union* (Stanford, Calif.: Stanford University Press, 1959).

7. Philip Mullenbach, *Civilian Nuclear Power* (New York: The Twentieth Century Fund, 1963).

8. U.S. Atomic Energy Commission, *Civilian Nuclear Power: A Report to the President* (Washington, D.C.: 1962).

9. Arturo Gandara, *Utility Decisionmaking and the Nuclear Option* (Santa Monica, Calif.: Rand Corporation, 1977).

10. R.L. Perry et al., *Development and Commercialization of the Light Water Reactor, 1946-1976* (Santa Monica, Calif.: Rand Corporation, 1977).

11. Irvin C. Bupp and Jean-Claude Derian, *Light Water: How the Nuclear Dream Dissolved*, (New York: Basic Books Inc., 1978).

12. Quoted in Bupp and Derian, *Light Water*.

13. William Walker and Måns Lönnroth, *Nuclear Power Struggles: Industrial Competition and Proliferation Control* (London: George Allen & Unwin, 1983); Peter Pringle and James Spigelman, *The Nuclear Barons* (New York: Holt, Rinehart & Winston, 1981).

14. James Everett Katz and Onkar S. Marwah, eds., *Nuclear Power in Develop-*
ing Countries (Lexington, Mass.: Lexington Books, 1982); Richard J. Barber
Associates, *LDC Nuclear Power Prospects, 1975-1990: Commercial, Economic and*
Security Implications (Washington, D.C.: 1974); Ziauddin Sardar, "Why the
Third World Needs Nuclear Power," *New Scientist*, February 12, 1981.

15. U.S. Atomic Industrial Forum, "International Survey—Annual," Washington, D.C., various years.

16. Quoted in Bupp and Derian, *Light Water*.

17. Cost figures for individual plants are compiled from press reports and
personal communications with utilities by Worldwatch Institute and are
current as of late 1983. All cost figures are in current (as spent) dollars unless
indicated otherwise.

18. The origin of this quote is a mystery, though some have attributed it to
Lewis Strauss, former chairman of the U.S. Atomic Energy Commission; see
Stephen Hilgartner, Richard C. Bell and Rory O'Connor, *Nukespeak* (San
Francisco: Sierra Club Books, 1982).

19. Perry et al., *Development and Commercialization of the Light Water Reactor*;
Bupp and Derian, *Light Water*.

20. Irvin C. Bupp et al., "Trends in Light Water Reactor Capital Costs in the
United States: Causes and Consequences," Center for Policy Alternatives,
Massachusetts Institute of Technology, December 1974.

21. Bupp et al., "Trends in Light Water Reactor Costs" and William E. Mooz,
Cost Analysis of Light Water Reactor Plants (Santa Monica, Calif.: Rand Corporation, 1978).

22. Industry studies showing a large cost advantage for nuclear power
include Lewis J. Perl, "Estimated Costs of Coal and Nuclear Generation,"
National Economic Research Associates, 1978, and W.K. Davis, "Economics
of Nuclear Power," Bechtel Power Corporation, San Francisco, 1981.

23. Charles Komanoff, *Power Plant Cost Escalation: Nuclear and Coal Capital*
Costs, Regulation and Economics (New York: Komanoff Energy Associates,
1981), republished by Van Nostrand Reinhold in 1983.

24. An industry analysis of cost trends in current dollars showing a 20
percent annual rate of increase through 1981 is found in Ramesh N. Budwani,
"Power Plant Scheduling, Construction and Costs: 10-Year Analysis," *Power*
Engineering, August 1982. A list of utility cost estimates for all nuclear plants

under construction as of mid-1983 was obtained from the Environmental Action Foundation. Constant dollar cost estimates are from the Komanoff Energy Associate's data base, private communication, September 19, 1983. These figures were confirmed by Richard Rosen using the data base of the Energy Systems Research Group, private communication, September 27, 1983.

25. Richard A. Rosen, "Testimony before the Indiana Public Service Commission," October 4, 1982, based on Energy Systems Research Group statistical data.

26. U.S. Department of Energy, *Annual Report to Congress, 1982* (Washington, D.C.: 1983); U.S. Department of Energy, *Statistical Data of the Uranium Industry* (Washington, D.C.: 1983).

27. R.G. Easterling, *Statistical Analysis of Power Plant Capacity Factors Through 1979* (Washington, D.C.: U.S. Nuclear Regulatory Commission, 1981); Steve Thomas, *Worldwide Nuclear Plant Performance Revisited: An Analysis of 1978-1981* (Brighton, U.K.: Science Policy Research Unit, 1983).

28. Richard Rosen, Energy Systems Research Group, private communication, September 27, 1983.

29. Some of the most misleading but most widely quoted cost figures are those published by the Atomic Industrial Forum in its annual fall press release comparing nuclear and coal generating costs; see Atomic Industrial Forum, "Nuclear Power Boosts Its Advantage Over Coal In Costs and Capacity Factor," press release, November 22, 1982. The AIF approach is dissected in Charles Komanoff, "Power Propaganda: A Critique of the Atomic Industrial Forum's Nuclear and Coal Power Cost Data for 1978," Environmental Action Foundation, March 1980. The AIF has responded to such criticism by no longer breaking down the data by plant in its press releases, making independent evaluation of the results impossible.

30. Lewis J. Perl, "The Economics of Nuclear Power," National Economic Research Associates, New York, June 3, 1982; Lewis J. Perl, "The Current Economics of Electric Generation from Coal in the U.S. and Western Europe," National Economic Research Associates, October 26, 1982.

31. U.S. Department of Energy, *Projected Costs of Electricity from Nuclear and Coal-Fired Power Plants* (Washington, D.C.: 1982).

32. These figures are Worldwatch Institute estimates based on the construction cost figures described earlier and on O&M and capacity factor figures compiled by Energy Systems Research Group and Komanoff Energy Associates. Oil prices are assumed to rise at a 3.5 percent annual real rate beginning in 1986 and hit $50 per barrel (1983 dollars) by the year 2000. Coal prices are assumed to rise at a 2 percent annual real rate and plants have "scrubbers" for SO_2 removal. Generating cost figures are levelized costs over the lifetime of a plant. Because two-thirds of nuclear generating costs are construction costs paid during the early years of operation, nuclear power appears even less attractive than the alternatives during the first years of operation.

33. Figure based on a nuclear generating cost of 11¢ per kilowatt-hour that, with transmission and distribution costs and line losses, comes to a delivered price of 14.3¢ per kilowatt-hour. This compares with a U.S. average retail electricity price in 1983 of 6.3¢ per kilowatt-hour, according to U.S. Department of Energy, *Monthly Energy Review,* September 1983.

34. Figure based on one barrel of oil equal in energy value to 1700 kilowatt-hours of electricity after refining.

35. S. David Freeman, "Nuclear Power Isn't Scary—These Reactors Are," *Washington Post*, November 28, 1982.

36. "Sizewell B Inquiry Puts UK Energy Policy on Trial," *European Energy Report*, September 16, 1983; Chad Neighbor, "Nukes and Crumpets," *Environmental Action*, June 1983.

37. Central Electricity Generating Board, *The Case for the Sizewell B Nuclear Power Station* (London: 1982); "British PWR Can Cut Costs," *Nuclear Engineering International*, June 1982; Gordon Mackerron, "Nuclear Power and the Economic Interests of Consumers," Electricity Consumers' Council, June 1982; Gordon Mackerron, "A Case Not Proven," *New Scientist*, January 13, 1983; J.W. Jeffery, "The Real Cost of Nuclear Electricity in the U.K.," *Energy Policy*, June 1982; J.W. Jeffery, "An Economic Critique of the CEGB's Statement of Case for a PWR at Sizewell," University of London, June 1983.

38. David Fishlock, "Counting the Real Cost of Nuclear Energy," *Financial Times*, August 9, 1982; "Sizewell B Inquiry," *European Energy Report*.

39. Gunter Marquis, "Experience with Nuclear Power Plant Investment Costs in the Federal Republic of Germany and Expected Future Electricity Production Costs," presented to the International Conference on Nuclear Power Experience, Vienna, Austria, September 13-17, 1982; Leonard L. Bennett, Panos M. Karousakis and Georges Moynet, "Review of Nuclear Power Costs Around the World," presented to the International Conference.

40. Jürgen Franke and Dieter Viefhues, *Das Ende Des Billigen Atomstroms* (Koln, West Germany: Institut Freiburg, 1983).

41. Bennett, Karousakis and Moynet, "Review of Nuclear Power Costs"; Charles Komanoff, "Nuclear Power Costs: American Answers, French Questions," Komanoff Energy Associates, 1981; "Even with Increased Costs, EDF Finds Nuclear Far Cheaper than Coal," *Nucleonics Week*, January 27, 1983.

42. "Electricité de France Spent 9.76-Billion Francs in 1981," *Nucleonics Week*, February 25, 1982; "EDF Reschedules Debt," *European Energy Report*, January 21, 1983.

43. The Japanese figures are unpublished estimates of the Central Research Institute of Electric Power Industry, private communication, August 9, 1983, and of the executive vice-president of Tokyo Electric Power Company in an interview in *Asiaweek*, August 12, 1983. The Soviet figure is from "Comecon Presses Forward While the West Hesitates," *Financial Times Energy Economist*, August 1983. The Swedish figure is from Åke Sundström, Ministry of Industry, private communication, September 12, 1983.

44. A.M. Yu and D.L.S. Bate, "Trends in the Capital Costs of CANDU Generating Stations," presented to the International Conference; Ontario Hydro, *Cost Comparison of CANDU Nuclear & Coal Fueled Generating Stations* (Toronto: 1982); Bennett, Karousakis and Moynet, "Review of Nuclear Power Costs."

45. Daniel Ford, *The Cult of the Atom* (New York: Simon & Schuster, 1982).

46. David Okrent, *Nuclear Reactor Safety: On the History of the Regulatory Process* (Madison, Wisc.: University of Wisconsin Press, 1981).

47. Bupp and Derian, *Light Water*.

48. Marquis, "Experience with Nuclear Power Plant Investment Costs in Germany."

49. Komanoff, *Power Plant Cost Escalation*.

50. Jim Mintz, "How the Engineers are Sinking Nuclear Power," *Science 83*, June 1983; Mark Evanoff, "Boondoggle at Diablo," *Not Man Apart*, September 1981.

51. Quoted in Komanoff, *Power Plant Cost Escalation*.

52. Marquis, "Experience with Nuclear Power Plant Investment Costs in Germany."

53. Ramesh N. Budwani, "Power Plant Scheduling, Construction and Costs: 10-Year Analysis," *Power Engineering*, August 1982; F.C. Olds, "Nuclear Power Engineering: Analysis of Trends in Policy and Technology," *Power Engineering*, March 1983.

54. Atomic Industrial Forum, "Licensing, Design and Construction Problems: Priorities for Solution," Washington, D.C., January 1978.

55. Komanoff, *Power Plant Cost Escalation*.

56. Management problems at U.S. nuclear projects are described in John F. Ahearne, "Remarks Before the American Nuclear Society," Cornell University, May 14, 1982, and Mintz, "How the Engineers are Sinking Nuclear Power."

57. Alvin Weinberg, "Nuclear Power After Three Mile Island," *Wilson Quarterly*, Spring 1980.

58. Matthew L. Wald, "The High Cost of Low-Cost Nuclear Power," *New York Times*, December 15, 1981.

59. Mark Hertsgaard, *Nuclear Inc.: The Men and Money Behind Nuclear Energy* (New York: Pantheon Books, 1983).

60. Remy Carle, "How France Went Nuclear," *New Scientist*, January 13, 1983; Irvin C. Bupp, "The French Nuclear Harvest: Abundant Energy or Bitter Fruit?" *Technology Review*, November/December 1980.

61. S. David Freeman, "Nuclear Power Isn't Scary—These Reactors Are," *Washington Post*, November 28, 1982; Peter A. Bradford, "Reagan and Nuclear Power," *Los Angeles Times*, June 6, 1982.

62. Statement made to Amory Lovins in 1981, private communication, October 14, 1983.

63. Ronnie D. Lipschutz, *Radioactive Waste: Politics, Technology and Risk* (Cambridge, Mass.: Ballinger Publishing Co., 1980); Fred C. Shapiro, *Radwaste: A Reporter's Investigation of a Growing Nuclear Menace* (New York: Random House, 1981).

64. U.S. Congress, Office of Technology Assessment, *Managing Commercial High-Level Radioactive Waste* (Washington, D.C.: 1982); Luther J. Carter, "The Radwaste Paradox," *Science*, January 7, 1983; Walter Sullivan, "Nuclear Waste Disposal: Bold Innovations Abroad," *New York Times*, August 31, 1982; U.S. Congress, *Nuclear Waste Policy Act of 1982* (Washington, D.C.: 1982).

65. Testimony by Henry Eschwage, U.S. General Accounting Office, before the Subcommittee on Conservation, Energy and Natural Resources of the Committee on Government Operations, February 23, 1976; Shapiro, *Radwaste*.

66. U.S. Department of Energy, *U.S. Commercial Nuclear Power* (Washington, D.C.: 1982); Richard Hellman and Caroline J.C. Hellman, *The Competitive Economics of Nuclear and Coal Power* (Lexington, Mass.: Lexington Books, 1982).

67. Fred Barbash and Milton R. Benjamin, "States Can Curb A-Plants: California Moratorium Upheld," *Washington Post*, April 21, 1983; John W. Powell, "Nuclear Power in Japan," *Bulletin of the Atomic Scientists*, May 1983.

68. Sally Hindman, *Decommissioning Policies for Nuclear Power Plants: A Critical Examination* (Washington, D.C.: Critical Mass, forthcoming); U.S. Nuclear Regulatory Commission, "Draft Environmental Impact Statement on Decommissioning of Nuclear Facilities," Washington, D.C., 1981; Atomic Industrial Forum, "An Overview of Decommissioning Nuclear Power Plants," Washington, D.C., 1983; Joseph A. Sefcik, "Decommissioning Commercial Nuclear Reactors," *Technology Review*, June/July 1979.

69. Colin Norman, "A Long-Term Problem for the Nuclear Industry," *Science*, January 12, 1982; Jim Harding, "The High Price of Burying Dead Reactors," *Not Man Apart*, December 1980; David F. Greenwood et al., *Analysis of Nuclear Reactor Decommissioning Costs*, (Washington, D.C.: Atomic Industrial Forum, 1981); Duane Chapman, *Nuclear Economics: Taxation, Fuel Costs and Decommissioning* (Sacramento, Calif.: California Energy Commission, 1980); "General Electric Has Won the $60 to $70-million Decommissioning Contract," *Nucleonics Week*, October 27, 1983.

70. West German figure from Florentin Krause, Friends of the Earth, private communication, September 28, 1983; Hindman, "Decommissioning Policies"; R.S. Wood, "Assuring the Availability of Funds for Decommissioning Nuclear Facilities," Nuclear Regulatory Commission, Washington, D.C., 1982; Robert F. Burns et al., *Funding Nuclear Power Plant Decommissioning* (Columbus, Ohio: Nuclear Regulatory Research Institute, 1982).

71. Atomic Industrial Forum, "Historical Profile of U.S. Nuclear Power Development," Washington, D.C., January 1983.

72. Atomic Industrial Forum, "Historical Profile"; update from Mary Ellen Warren, Atomic Industrial Forum, private communication, October 26, 1983; coal plant data from Atomic Industrial Forum, "Interoffice Memorandum," March 22, 1983.

73520

73. Cost figures are in current dollars and are from U.S. Department of Energy, *Nuclear Plant Cancellations: Causes, Costs, and Consequences* (Washington, D.C.: 1983).

74. U.S. Department of Energy, *Monthly Energy Review*, September 1983; "33rd Annual Electrical Industry Forecast," *Electrical World*, September 1982; U.S. General Accounting Office, *Analysis of Electric Utility Load Forecasting* (Washington, D.C.: 1983); U.S. Department of Energy, *The Future of Electric Power in America: Economic Supply for Economic Growth* (Washington, D.C.: 1983).

75. "1983 Annual Statistical Report," *Electrical World*, March 1983. Additional data was obtained from unpublished documents of the Edison Electric Institute and the American Public Power Association. These numbers were compared with capital expenditure figures in U.S. Bureau of the Census, *Annual Survey of Manufacturers* (Washington, D.C.: 1983).

76. U.S. Department of Energy, *Future of Electric Power*.

77. Leonard Hyman, "Utility Industry: Congressional Hearings on Nuclear Energy," Merrill Lynch, Pierce, Fenner & Smith Inc., New York, October 26, 1981; R.J. Nesse, "The Effect of Nuclear Ownership on Utility Bond Ratings and Yields," Battelle Pacific Northwest Laboratory, Richland, Washington, February 1982. The initial rate increases that occur when nuclear plants begin generating power are higher in real terms than the lifetime generating cost of the plant. This is because the capital cost of the plants must be repaid during the first 10-15 years of operation.

78. John R. Emshwiller, "Some Investors Shun Nuclear-Powered Utilities, Jeopardizing Funds to Build New Atomic Plants," *Wall Street Journal*, November 20, 1983.

79. Scott A. Fenn, *America's Electric Utilities: Under Siege and in Transition* (Washington, D.C.: Investor Responsibility Research Center, 1983); Thomas Watterson, "Generating Capital: Utilities Look to Rest of the Century," *Christian Science Monitor*, July 28, 1983.

80. "Midland Deal Comes Unglued," *Energy Daily*, July 19, 1983.

81. U.S. Department of Energy, *Monthly Energy Review*, September 1983. Individual rate requests are from various sources, including "Economic Factors Engulf Seabrook," *New York Times*, September 12, 1983. The initial rate increases that occur when nuclear plants begin generating power are higher in real terms than the lifetime generating cost of the plant. This is because the capital cost of the plants must be repaid during the first 10-15 years of operation.

82. The argument in favor of granting large rate increases is made in Peter Navarro, "Utility Bills: The Real Price of Electricity," *Wall Street Journal*, January 13, 1983 and Sam Glasser, "Electricity Pricing Needs New Attitudes by State Regulators," *Journal of Commerce*, December 6, 1982. The argument for making investors bear more of the cost of overruns is made in Charles Komanoff, "Nuclear Cost Overruns: Make Investors Share the Burden," *Power Line*, March 1983 and Mark Evanoff, "Huge Costs Shake Utility Financing," *Not Man Apart*, July 8, 1983.

83. Stuart Diamond, "Shoreham: What Went Wrong?," *Newsday*, December 6, 1981; James Barron, "Burden of Lilco Bills Could Slow Up Long Island's Economy," *New York Times*, August 14, 1983; Ron Winslow, "Lilco's Bid to Spread Nuclear Costs Riles Customers and State Officials," *Wall Street Journal*, September 1, 1983; Matthew L. Wald, "Operating Shoreham Power Plant Will Not Lower Rates, Study Says," *New York Times*, October 14, 1983.

84. Tamar Lewin, "Power Group Says It Cannot Pay Off $2.25 Billion Debt," *New York Times*, July 26, 1983; Michael Blumstein, "The Lessons of a Bond Failure," *New York Times*, August 14, 1983; Scott Ridley, "Nuclear Power Bankrupts the Northwest," *Environmental Action*, July/August 1983.

85. "The Fallout from 'Whoops': A Default Looms, Casting a Pall Over the Entire Municipal Market," *Business Week*, July 1983.

86. Joseph Bowring, *Federal Subsidies to Nuclear Power: Reactor Design and the Fuel Cycle* (Washington, D.C.: U.S. Department of Energy, 1981); U.S. General Accounting Office, *Nuclear Power Costs and Subsidies* (Washington, D.C.: 1979).

87. Duane Chapman, "The 1981 Tax Act and the Economics of Coal and Nuclear Power," Cornell Agricultural Economics Staff Paper, Ithaca, New York, October 1981; Duane Chapman, "Nuclear Economics: Taxation, Fuel Cost and Decommissioning," California Energy Commission, Sacramento, California, 1980.

88. "We Wuz Robbed: The Nuclear Industry is Stealing Our Tax Dollars," *Environmental Action*, June 1983.

89. U.S. Department of Energy, *Nuclear Plant Cancellations*.

90. Keiki Kehoe, *Nuclear Insurance: Unavailable at Any Price* (Washington, D.C.: Environmental Policy Center, 1980); Matthew L. Wald, "Reactors May Lose Limit on Liability," *New York Times*, July 27, 1983.

91. Atomic Industrial Forum, "A.I.F.'s 1982 Midyear Outlook," Washington, D.C., July 1982.

92. U.S. Department of Energy, *U.S. Commercial Nuclear Power: Historical Perspective, Current Status and Outlook* (Washington, D.C.: 1982).

93. Quoted in Hertsgaard, *Nuclear Inc.*

94. "World List of Nuclear Power Plants," *Nuclear News*, bi-annual, various dates; Organisation for Economic Co-operation and Development, *World Energy Outlook*.

95. William Walker and Måns Lönnroth, *Nuclear Power Struggles: Industrial Competition and Proliferation Control* (London: George Allen & Unwin, 1983).

96. William Drozdiak, "Greens' Power: West German Party Forces Nuclear Issue," *Washington Post*, February 19, 1983; John Tagliabue, "West Germans Clash At Site of A-Plant," *New York Times*, March 1, 1981.

97. Heinz Günter Kemmer, "Era of Cheap Electricity Coming to an End," *German Tribune*, August 22, 1982; "Regenerating the Nuclear Option," *World Business Weekly*, February 23, 1981.

98. "West Germany Breaks Through Five Years of Paper Chains," *Financial Times Energy Economist*, September 1982; Walker and Lonnroth, *Nuclear Power Struggles*.

99. "West Germany: Can a Nuclear 'Convoy' Run Over Its Opposition?" *Business Week*, August 9, 1982. Information on concern within the West German utility industry is from Florentin Krause, Friends of the Earth, private communication, September 28, 1983.

100. "World List of Nuclear Power Plants," *Nuclear News*; International Atomic Energy Agency, *The Annual Report for 1982*.

101. Carole Collins, "Framatome: French Nuclear Monopoly Finds Fertile Ground Abroad," *Multinational Monitor*, July 1983; "Creusot-Loire to Reduce Stake in Framatome," *Wall Street Journal*, October 4, 1983.

102. Irvin C. Bupp, "The French Nuclear Harvest: Abundant Energy or Bitter Harvest?" *Technology Review*, November/December 1980; Judith Miller, "Paris Pushes Drive for Atomic Energy: Socialist Government Has Only Slightly Changed Program Undertaken by Giscard," *New York Times*, March 14, 1982; David Fishlock, "The Future for French Nuclear Power," *Financial Times*, August 25, 1982.

103. "French Energy: Forecasts Fall," *Nature*, November 11, 1982; "Study Group's Call for French Nuclear Retrenchment Sends Shock Waves,"

Nucleonics Week, May 19, 1983; "Nuclear Power: Cooling Off," *The Economist*, July 30, 1983; "French Planners Accused of Cheating," *European Energy Report*, September 30, 1983; "EDF Seeking Maximum Flexibility in Operation of Its Nuclear Units," *Nucleonics Week*, February 17, 1983.

104. "France: Nuclear Over-Capacity Even Before 1985," *European Energy Report*, July 1, 1983; "EDF Faces Big Task in Reprogramming Industry to Use More Electricity," *Nucleonics Week*, March 4, 1982.

105. "Electricité de France Spent 9.76-Billion Francs in 1981," *Nucleonics Week*, February 25, 1982; "EDF Reschedules Debt," *European Energy Report*, January 21, 1983; "Nuclear Power: Cooling Off," *The Economist*, July 30, 1983.

106. "Study Group's Call for French Nuclear Retrenchment Sends Shock Waves," *Nucleonics Week*, May 19, 1983; "France Eases Up on Pace of N-Power," *European Energy Report*, August 5, 1983; "Framatome is Bracing for Employment Problems Beginning in Mid-1984," *Nucleonics Week*, November 4, 1983; "Slowed Rhythm of French Ordering to Force Nuclear Plant Prices Up," *Nucleonics Week*, April 21, 1983.

107. Walker and Lonnroth, *Nuclear Power Struggles*.

108. Andrew Holmes, "Sizewell Inquiry Reveals U.K. Policy Vacuum," *Financial Times Energy Economist*, October 1983; Czech Conroy, "Why Britain Does Not Need a PWR," *New Scientist*, August 19, 1982.

109. Andrew Holmes, "Nuclear: World Status, *Financial Times Energy Economist*, January 1983.

110. "Sweden Proposes Phasing Out Its Nuclear Power Plants," *World Environment Report*, April 27, 1981; Thomas Land, "Sweden Counts Nuclear Power's Real Cost," *Journal of Commerce*, March 4, 1983.

111. U.S. Congress, Office of Technology Assessment, *Technology & Soviet Energy Availability*, (Washington, D.C.: 1981); Leslie Dienes and Theodore Shabad, *The Soviet Energy System: Resource Use and Policies* (Washington, D.C.: V.H. Winston & Sons, 1979); "Comecon Nuclear Industry Set for Rapid Expansion," *European Energy Report*, July 8, 1983.

112. Peter Wood, "Nuclear Power in Eastern Europe," *The Ecologist*, January 1980; Peter Holt, "Nuclear Power in Eastern Europe: Progress & Problems," *Energy in Countries with Planned Economies*, December 1981; Tom Sealy, "Comecon Presses Forward," *Financial Times Energy Economist*, August 1983.

113. "Comecon Presses Forward," *Financial Times Energy Economist;* "Problems Hit U.S.S.R. Nuclear Construction Industry," *European Energy Report,* August 5, 1983; Mark Wood, "Reactor Plant Mishap Hinted at by Soviets," *Washington Post,* July 21, 1983.

114. "Comecon Nuclear Industry Set For Rapid Expansion," *European Energy Report,* July 8, 1983.

115. John W. Powell, "Nuclear Power in Japan," *Bulletin of the Atomic Scientists,* May 1983; "Nuclear Power: What Role in Asia?," *Asiaweek,* August 12, 1983.

116. "Nuclear Suppliers Cater to Japanese Needs As They Wait Out Lull in U.S. Demand," *Electric Light and Power,* June 1982; "Japan: The Unlikely Nuclear Giant," *Business Week,* September 19, 1983; "Japan a Closed Shop for Outsiders; Japanese Face Same Problem Offshore," *Nucleonics Week,* May 5, 1983.

117. "A Nuclear Power Plant in Japan Springs a Radioactive Leak," *World Business Weekly,* May 11, 1981; Henry Scott Stokes, "For Japan, Sudden Nuclear Misgivings," *New York Times,* May 17, 1981; Geoffrey Murray, "Sub Crash, Waste Leak Shake Japan's Trust in A-Power, *Christian Science Monitor,* April 23, 1981; "Protest Demonstrations Mark Gov't Hearing on New N-Plants," *Japan Times,* December 5, 1980.

118. Steve Thomas, "Worldwide Nuclear Plant Performance Revisited: An Analysis of 1979-81," *Futures,* December 1982; "Japanese Nuclear Power Plants Have Experienced Relatively Few Problems," *Nucleonics Week,* July 17, 1983; Paul Danish, "Japan Delays Building of Coal-Fired Plants," *Journal of Commerce,* October 28, 1983; "Energy Forecasts from Tokyo Suggest Growing Uncertainty," *Financial Times Energy Economist,* July 1982; "Latest Revision of Japanese Nuclear Program Calls for Nearly $80-Billion," *Nucleonics Week,* July 1, 1982.

119. International Atomic Energy Agency, *Market Survey for Nuclear Power in Developing Countries: General Report* (Vienna: 1973).

120. "World List of Nuclear Power Plants," *Nuclear News,* August 1983; Jane House, "The Third World Goes Nuclear," *South,* December 1980.

121. Richard J. Barber Associates, *LDC Nuclear Power Prospects, 1975-1990: Commercial, Economic & Security Implications* (Washington, D.C.: U.S. Energy Research and Development Administration, 1975).

122. Richard J. Barber Associates, *LDC Nuclear Power Prospects*; Patrick O'Heffernan, Amory B. Lovins and L. Hunter Lovins, *The First Nuclear World War* (New York: William Morrow and Company Inc., 1983).

123. John J. Metzler, "Taiwan Extends Quest for Nuclear Power," *Journal of Commerce*, March 8, 1982; "Taiwan Power Delays Two Nuclear Projects," *Wall Street Journal*, July 13, 1982.

124. "KEPCO Shelving Construction of Nos. 11, 12 Nuclear Power Plants," *Korea Herald*, July 17, 1982; Namiki Nozomi, "South Korea: The Nuclear Industry's Last Hurrah," *AMPO: Japan-Asia Quarterly Review*, Vol 13, No. 1, 1981; Tim Shorrock, "Evaluation of Nuclear Power in South Korea," *Corporate Accountability Research Group*, 1983, unpublished.

125. S. Jacob Scherr, "Nuclear Power in the Philippines," in Katz and Marwah, *Nuclear Power in Developing Countries*.

126. Bernard Gwertzman, "U.S. and China Discussing Export of Nuclear Technology to Peking," *New York Times*, June 2, 1982; Christopher S. Wren, "China Is Building Atom Power Plant," *New York Times*, September 30, 1982; "Expansion of Nuclear Power Will Meet Needs," *China Daily*, October 16, 1982; Milton R. Benjamin, "Westinghouse Seeks Nuclear Sale to China," *Washington Post*, December 16, 1982; "U.K. and France Get Footholds in Chinese Nuclear Program," *Nucleonics Week*, March 31, 1983.

127. R.R. Subramanian and C. Raja Mohan, "Nuclear Power in India," in Katz and Marwah, *Nuclear Power in Developing Countries*; Trevor Drieberg, "India's Nuclear Program Encountering Difficulties," *Journal of Commerce*, November 4, 1982; R.K. Pachauri and Rashmi Pachauri, "India Seeks New Solutions to Primitive Problems," *Financial Times Energy Economist*, June 1983.

128. Katz and Marwah, *Nuclear Power in Developing Countries*; House, "The Third World Goes Nuclear"; Muriel Allen, "Egypt Rethinking Plans for Reactors Due to Safety Fears," *Journal of Commerce*, May 5, 1981.

129. Burt Solomon, "Argentina: Bent on a Home-Grown Nuclear Program," *Energy Daily*, November 9, 1982; Jackson Diehl, "Ambitious Argentine Nuclear Development Program Hits Snags," *Washington Post*, August 31, 1982; Jeremy Morgan, "Argentine Nuke Program Proceeds," *Journal of Commerce*, May 13, 1983.

130. Victoria Johnson, "Nuclear Power in Brazil," in Katz and Marwah, *Nuclear Power in Developing Countries*; Richard House, "Brazil: Nuclear Road to the Future Takes a Turn for the Worse," *Financial Times Energy Economist*, May 1983.

131. Juan Eibenschutz, "Nuclear Power in Mexico," in Katz and Marwah, *Nuclear Power in Developing Countries*; "Mexico Having Difficulty Completing Even One Nuclear Unit," *Nucleonics Week*, June 23, 1983.

132. Estimate based on nuclear plants under construction and operating in mid-1983 as listed in "World List of Nuclear Power Plants," *Nuclear News*, August 1983.

133. O'Heffernan, Lovins and Lovins, *The First Nuclear World War*.

134. *Ibid.*

135. Hobart Rowen, "Nuclear Reactors: Fear of Losing Export Race," *Washington Post*, May 17, 1981; "France: A Two-Pronged Spur for Nuclear Reactors," *Business Week*, February 23, 1981; Gloria C. Duffy and Gordon Adams, *Power Politics: The Nuclear Industry and Nuclear Exports* (New York: Council on Economic Priorities, 1978); Peter Hayes and Tim Shorrock, "Dumping Reactors in Asia: The U.S. Export-Import Bank and Nuclear Power in South Korea," *AMPO: Japan-Asia Quarterly Review*, Vol. 14, No. 1, 1983; Kaign Smith, "Atoms for the Poor, Cash for the Rich," *Ecoforum*, December 1982.

136. Atomic Industrial Forum, annual press releases on international outlook, various years; Nuclear Energy Agency, *Nuclear Energy and Its Fuel Cycle* (Paris: Organisation for Economic Co-operation and Development, 1982).

137. U.S. Department of Energy, *Monthly Energy Review*, September 1983.

138. The costs of pollution controls for coal-fired power plants are discussed in detail in Komanoff, *Power Plant Cost Escalation*. Ross Howard and Michael Perley, *Acid Rain* (New York: McGraw-Hill, Inc., 1982); Swedish Ministry of Agriculture, *Acidification Today and Tomorrow* (Stockholm: 1982); Council on Environmental Quality, *Global Energy Futures and the Carbon Dioxide Problem* (Washington, D.C.: 1979).

139. Solar Energy Research Institute, *A New Prosperity: Building a Renewable Future* (Andover, Mass.: Brick House, 1981); Northwest Power Planning Council, *Northwest Conservation and Electric Power Plan* (Portland, Oregon: 1983); David Olivier and Hugh Miall, *Energy Efficient Futures: Opening the Solar Option* (London: Earth Resources Research, 1983).

140. Howard S. Geller, *Energy Efficient Appliances* (Washington, D.C.: American Council for an Energy-Efficient Economy, 1983).

141. Worldwatch Institute estimate based on various sources.

142. Roger W. Sant and Dennis W. Bakke, *Creating Energy Abundance* (New York: McGraw-Hill, Inc. forthcoming).

143. Douglas Cogan, *Generating Energy Alternatives At America's Electric Utilities* (Washington, D.C.: Investor Responsibility Research Center Inc., 1983).

144. W.R.Z. Willey, "Alternative Energy Systems for Pacific Gas and Electric Company: An Economic Analysis," prepared testimony before the California Public Utilities Commission, San Francisco, 1978; Pacific Gas and Electric Company's plans as reformulated in the early eighties are described in Pacific Gas and Electric Company, "Long-Term Planning Results: 1982-2002," San Francisco, June 1982; Don Jordan is quoted in Douglas Cogan, *Generating Energy Alternatives*. For a detailed discussion of new utility strategies see Scott A. Fenn, *America's Electric Utilities*.

145. Electricity trends are from International Energy Agency, *World Energy Outlook*, and reports in various newsletters.

146. Renewable energy cost figures are Worldwatch Institute estimates based on various sources. See Daniel Deudney and Christopher Flavin, *Renewable Energy: The Power to Choose* (New York: W.W. Norton & Co., 1983).

147. Douglas Cogan, *Generating Energy Alternatives*.

148. "The Vicious Circle That Utilities Can't Seem To Break," *Business Week*, May 23, 1983.

149. International Energy Agency, *Energy Research, Development and Demonstration in the IEA countries, 1981 Review of National Programmes* (Paris: Organisation for Economic Co-operation and Development, 1982).

150. William Mooz and Sidney Siegel, *A Comparison of the Capital Costs of Light Water Reactor and Liquid Metal Fast Breeder Reactor Power Plants* (Santa Monica, Calif.: Rand Corportation, 1979); "Cheap Uranium Dampens Fast Breeder Interest," *Financial Times Energy Economist*, December 1981; David Dickson, "Europe's Fast Breeders Move to a Slow Track," *Science*, December 10, 1982; Dominique Finon, "Fast Breeder Reactors: The End of a Myth?" *Energy Policy*, December 1982.

151. "Penalty Set for Utilities with Balky A-Plants," *San Francisco Chronicle*, September 8, 1982.

CHRISTOPHER FLAVIN is a Senior Researcher with Worldwatch Institute and coauthor of *Renewable Energy: The Power to Choose* (W. W. Norton, Spring 1983). His research deals with renewable energy technologies and policies. He is a graduate of Williams College, where he studied Economics and Biology and participated in the Environmental Studies Program.

THE WORLDWATCH PAPER SERIES

No. of
Copies

Single Copy—$2.00

Bulk Copies (any combination of titles)
2-10: $1.50 each   11-50: $1.25 each   51 or more: $1.00 each

Calendar Year Subscription (1983 subscription begins with Paper 53)
$25.00 _____

Make check payable to Worldwatch Institute
1776 Massachusetts Avenue NW, Washington, D.C. 20036 USA

Enclosed is my check for U.S. $ _____

_____
name
_____
address
_____
city   **state**   **zip/country**